BAY AREA BY DESIGN

An Insider's Guide to a San Francisco Decorator's Secret Sources

by Kay Evans

TEN SPEED PRESS
Berkeley | Toronto

Ten Speed Press
PO Box 7123
Berkeley, California 94707
www.tenspeed.com

Distributed in Australia by Simon and Schuster Australia, in Canada by Ten Speed Press Canada, in New Zealand by Southern Publishers Group, in South Africa by Real Books, and in the United Kingdom and Europe by Airlift Book Company.

Cover and text design by Katy Brown
Author photo by Bob Concannon

Library of Congress Cataloging-in-Publication Data on file with the publisher.

Printed in the Unites States of America

First printing 2006
1 2 3 4 5 6 7 8 9 10 — 09 08 07 06

CONTENTS

F

G

H

I

K

L

ACKNOWLEDGMENTS

There are many friends and interior designers who assisted me with this labor of love by opening their hearts and generously sharing their secret sources. You know who you are and I thank you! I must, however, single out several very special colleagues, especially my good friend Bob Hogan, who not only shared his sources, but who also chauffeured me around the city for days on end while I was visiting sources and verifying information. Thanks to good friends and interior designers par excellence Paul Vincent Wiseman of The Wiseman Group, Suzanne Tucker of Tucker & Marks, Betsy Jaques, owner of Buy Design, and antiquarian Ed Hardy of Ed Hardy San Francisco, who bigheartedly opened their file drawers and resources to me. Jane MacLain kindly donated hours of editing, and finally, Bob Carrau Jr., who was relentless in not allowing me to give up on the idea I had for this book. I thank all of you with all my heart!

FOREWORD

Kay and I have been friends for many years. With her impeccable eye for detail, Kay has researched and developed this book. Her caring for her clients makes this a unique resource for anyone who has designed a home or who is working to make their home better, because at some point everyone has to ask . . . where do I go now?

A designer is only as good as his or her resources. I have been in the business for over thirty years and, for more than twenty-five of these, I have owned my own interior design firm. Believe me, I know what it takes to be successful, and that includes having great resources at hand!

Often, after finishing a project, we designers are drawn into the small details of maintaining the very home we created. This can be a costly nuisance for both the client and the designer. So pick up Kay's book, then dial! What a relief!

Paul Vincent Wiseman
San Francisco, California

TAKE IT FROM ME

The free-wheeling spirit of San Francisco and its environs has always drawn vibrant and resourceful men and women to its heart and continues to attract and nurture more than its share of unusually talented individuals today. Those of us who are lucky enough to live here take pride in our neighbors and our neighborhoods, places fairly bursting at the seams with a long history of artistic élan.

It has been my privilege to be part of this creative community as an interior designer since 1980. Maintaining my precious contacts has always been a priority for me. As I was preparing to join the 21st century by transferring the contents of my handwritten Rolodex to my new computer, my thoughts kept returning to the years (and years) it took me to cultivate all my special sources.

As my twenty-fifth anniversary as a designer approached, I asked myself how I could give back to the community of artisans and craftspeople who have made my life's work possible, and how I could contribute to the greater community in which I have lived so happily for so long. The answer was to make my "secret" sources available, not just to friends or colleagues, but to everyone fortunate enough to call the Bay Area home.

All the resources listed within these pages are my own or were given to me by other designers, architects, contractors, or friends whose judgment I trust. I have neither charged nor accepted any fees for their inclusion. Should you choose to use any of the sources offered here, and I hope you do, please don't hesitate to relate your experiences to me. If you have a favorite trusted resource that you would like to share with me, I'd love to hear from you. I hope my little book will serve you well!

—Kay Evans

Have nothing in your home

that you do not know to be useful,

or do not believe to be beautiful.

—William Morris

APPLIANCE / ELECTRONICS REPAIR & RESTORATION

A-PLUS ELECTRONICS INC.
2111 Van Ness Avenue • San Francisco, CA 94109
415-474-2111

Michael Braude has been repairing TVs, VCRs, camcorders, and stereos since 1990. He recently merged with Ken Ma, who services computers and other electronics and together they will make quite a team. Open Monday through Friday 10 to 6 and Saturday 10 to 5. And they even make house calls.

BUCKEYE APPLIANCE
714 W. Fremont Street • Stockton, CA 95203
209-464-9643 • www.buckeyeappliance.com

Opened by Tom Lawson in 1976 as an appliance repair shop (aptly named by this loyal supporter of the Ohio State Buckeyes), in 1986 the store added an antique appliance restoration service. Today, Tom specializes in working vintage stoves for repair or resale, so if you're looking for a period stove, or have one to sell, this is the place to go.

ELECTRIC EURO SERVICE
1913 Salvio • Concord, CA 94520
925-687-1442

Established in 1974, Original owner. Electric Euro services and/or repairs vacuum cleaners, electric shavers, lamps and lighting fixtures, mixers, food processors, power tools, and "almost anything that has a cord on it."

GOURMET DEPOT

840 Folsom Street • San Francisco, CA 94107
415-777-5241 • www.thegourmetdepotco.com

No, not an upscale grocery, Gourmet Depot employs talented technicians who can repair just about anything electrical. In business since 1954, Gourmet Depot sells reconditioned small appliances, unusual and hard-to-find items, factory re-boxed merchandise at dramatically reduced prices, and more than 21,000 spare parts.

PHIL'S ELECTRIC VACUUM CENTER

2701 Lombard Street • San Francisco, CA 94123
415-921-3776 • www.philselectric.com

Originally started in 1941, Phil and his wife purchased the business in 1979 and moved it to its present location near the Presidio in 1982. They offer specialized repairs for vacuums, shavers, lamps and small appliances. They also carry off-brand hard-to-find bags (which is what led me to Phil's) and stock a range of specialty cleaning products for marble, hardwood floors, stainless steel, etc. Open Monday through Saturday 9 to 5:30.

UNIVERSAL ELECTRIC SERVICE

1551 Clement Street • San Francisco, CA 94118
415-386-5700

A small shop with a big reputation for quality service, owner Son Nguyen does all repair work and lamp rewiring himself. In business since 1975, Universal Electric also sells reconditioned items at a substantial discount, as well as servicing and selling parts for all makes of vacuum cleaners, shavers, clippers, and rice cookers.

ARBORIST

PROFESSIONAL TREE CARE
806 44th Avenue • San Francisco, CA 94121
415-823-9714

Landscape architects have been referring Dean Shreiner to their clients since 1979 because he approaches his work with an artistic eye as well as practical experience. In addition to pruning, Dean supervises tree installation and consults on garden design. Customized for the diverse Bay Area microclimates. By appointment.

TREE SHAPERS
415-239-2420 • www.treeshapers.com

Ted Kipping and Phil Danielson work with homeowners, landscape architects, and property management companies and will tackle trees and shrubs less than ten feet tall to over one hundred feet tall. Ted is frequently in demand as a consultant and lecturer in arboriculture and plant health care. Call for a consultation.

ARCHITECTURAL MODELS

GIMMITI MODEL ART
2169 Folsom • San Francisco, CA 94110
415-252-7536 • www.gimmiti.com

Architectural models have been used for thousands of years to understand and perceive structures multi-dimensionally. Once reserved for commercial construction projects, hiring a model maker has become a basic necessity for many architects and interior designers working on complex residential projects. Lisa Gimmiti has always been passionate about building scale models and, with more than twenty-five years experience, is considered to be tops in her field. By appointment.

ARCHITECTURAL SALVAGE

OHMEGA SALVAGE
2407 San Pablo Avenue • Berkeley, CA 94702
510-843-7368 • www.ohmegasalvage.com

Since 1974, specialized in architectural materials salvaged from buildings dating from the Victorian era through the 1940s. Visiting Ohmega Salvage is an adventure not for the faint-hearted. You'll find row upon row of interior and exterior doors, windows, shutters, cast and wrought iron gates, railings and fencing, sinks, tubs and commodes, stained glass, stone garden statuary, miscellaneous fixtures and hardware, as well as marvelous wood and plaster architectural components.

OMEGA TOO
2204 San Pablo Avenue • Berkeley, CA 94702
510-204-0767 • www.omegatoo.com

Omega Too is an annex Ohmega Salvage. They specialize in a sophisticated inventory of restored antiques as well as reproduction lighting, shades, bathroom fixtures, and interior accessories.

RESTORE
9235 San Leandro Street • Oakland, CA 94609
510-777-1447 • www.restorecommunity.com

Run by East Bay Habitat for Humanity as a fundraising arm of its affordable house building efforts, ReStore is a depository for new and used building materials. Their inventory is usually donated overstock from large manufacturers or single items purchased by contractors but rejected by their clients. Generally, the merchandise is new, however the occasional vintage piece sneaks in. They have a large selection of doors, tubs, sinks, assorted appliances, windows and hardware.

ART, APPRAISAL

JOHN ANGUS MCKENZIE
415-391-5997

John McKenzie spent the first thirty years of his career in Great Britain before moving to the U.S. in 1985, where he has been appraising art and antiques ever since. He specializes in eighteenth and nineteenth century furniture, paintings, silver, sculpture and rugs. John has a large personality and the expertise to match. By appointment.

ART CONSERVATION & RESTORATION, PAINTING

CLAIRE ANTONETTI
3242 Morcom Avenue • Oakland, CA 94619 • 510-535-1663

With degrees in art history and library preservation administration, Claire is expert in restoring works on paper and on canvas. Claire has worked with Conservation Art Services for more than a decade and additionally enjoys working with owners of large art collections making assessments and recommendations for display lighting and/or storage. By appointment.

CONSERVATION OF ART
Jim Pennuto
324 Lang Road • Burlingame, CA 94010
650-548-0560 • jamescoa@earthlink.net

Since 1968, offering conservation, preservation and restoration of paintings, works of art on paper and objects including ceramics, glass, enamels, and period frames. All services follow the guidelines of the American Institute For Conservation of Historic and Artistic Works. All their treatments are documented, including any materials and chemicals used, and available to the client for insurance claims, estate planning, etc. By appointment.

LIDA SCARBOROUGH

816 Kansas • San Francisco, CA 94107 • 415-824-1919

Originally from Prague, Lida Scarborough brought her European restoration techniques to San Francisco in 1987. She has been cleaning and restoring oil paintings, gouaches, watercolors, prints (and repairing and restoring the antique frames around them, if needed) ever since. Probably best known for her proficiency in color matching and seamless touch-up, Lida has a first-rate reputation with auction houses, galleries, art dealers, as well as her many private clients. By appointment.

ART CONSERVATION & RESTORATION, PAPER

ANITA NOENNIG

2121 Peralta, Studio 182 • Oakland, CA 94601 • 510-625-1645

In 1975, after receiving degrees in printmaking and art history, Anita embarked on a career as a conservator of works on paper, including rare documents, photographs, maps, and letters. Conservation and preservation not only enhance the appearance of an aging and fragile paper document, they may be crucial for its survival and even prolong its life span. Anita is available by appointment and since she is on the referral lists of many local museums, her schedule fills up quickly. She is also available for lectures on conservation and preservation concerns.

KAREN ZUKOR

3016 Filbert #10 • Oakland, CA 94608 • 510-652-7915

Karen specializes in works on paper, including manuscripts, watercolors, maps, documents, letters, drawings, books, Oriental paper screens and scrolls, and fine poster art. She is able to work with large items that other conservationists may not have the facilities to handle. She also enjoys working on location with historic wallpapers in need of her skills. Karen consults with a number of museums and libraries, conducts workshops and lectures on paper restoration and conservation. By appointment.

ART, CONSULTANT

EDITH CALDWELL
819 Bridgeway • Sausalito, CA 94965 • 415-331-5003

A great art consultant is one that is wildly passionate about their chosen field. One of these is Edie Caldwell. Edie represents many fine artists, has great contacts in the art world, and, after learning your personal tastes and interests, will guide you to just the right galleries and dealers. Stop by her gallery or call for an appointment.

LAURIE GHIELMETTI INTERIORS
4670 Willow Road, Suite 200 • Pleasanton, CA 94588
925-416-8084

Laurie will be the consummate guide on your quest for quality fine art for your home or office. You will enjoy every minute with this extremely bright, articulate woman and receive a "total immersion course" in art history along the way. Laurie will visit you in your home or office first for a consultation, and then plan an outing to visit local galleries together. By appointment.

SUZANNE STRID
95 Beach Road • Belvedere, CA 94921 • 415-889-4087

Suzanne is a consultant specializing exclusively in California art. Her clients are knowledgeable private collectors who enjoy having fine art in their homes but at the same time are savvy art investors. Suzanne works with dealers throughout the United States and watches the national art market very carefully. She also enjoys working with those who are new to the auction scene and anxious to try their hand at it. For a fee Suzanne will accompany clients for a day at a local auction house, assisting them with item assessment and the protocols for on-site and absentee bidding. By appointment.

ART, FRAMING

ARCADIA FRAMING
680 Eighth Street • San Francisco, CA 94103
415-551-1238 • www.arcadiaframing.com

Arcadia Framing has been providing custom framing since 1991, working primarily with the design trade. They pride themselves on offering conservation and preservation framing techniques according to the standards set by the Bay Area Art Conservation Guild, of which they are members. Many of their frames are one of a kind.

ART FOR ART
2786 Diamond Street • San Francisco, CA 94131 • 415-333-3344

Walter Fredrick started his framing business in the mid-1980s when, as an artist himself, he needed frames for his own paintings. Word of mouth spread the news of his expertise and special eye. Today, he creates designs and custom frames for collectors and decorators in his shop in Glen Park. He also does expert gilding and skilled antique frame repair.

CADRE
840 Sansome Street • San Francisco, CA 94111
415-296-0400 • www.cadre-sf.com

Known for museum-quality framing services, Hiedi Knodle and her staff receive framing commissions from all over the country. They carry beautiful reproduction frames in a variety of historical styles as well as an exclusive line designed and created exclusively for them. Cadre is also able to customize the perfect "period" frame from scratch if need be. In addition, they offer antique frame repair and they ship all over the United States.

FRAMING INTERIORS

1325 Fourth Street • San Rafael, CA 94901 • 415-460-0278

Owner Steve Mack ran a successful framing business in San Francisco for twenty-four years before making a move to San Rafael in 2003. His loyal customers have followed him there because Steve does all the work himself and will custom-frame everything from your child's first finger painting to family heirlooms to museum-worthy masterpieces.

MICHAEL W. PERRY & COMPANY

1837 Divisadero • San Francisco, CA 94115 • 415-563-8853

Over the course of more than twenty years of collecting antique prints and maps, Michael Perry learned how to build frames. When, in 2004, he had the opportunity to open his own workshop on Divisadero Street, he grabbed it. In addition to prints, drawings, photographs and other art on paper, he enjoys the challenge of framing three-dimensional objects, i.e. collages or small antiques, using only museum-quality framing materials and techniques,

PAIGE GLASS

(See Glass & Mirrors)

THE PAINTERS PLACE

317 Hayes Street • San Francisco, CA 94103
415-431-9827 • framing@thepaintersplace.com
—and—
1825 Eastshore Highway • Berkeley, CA 94710 • 510-843-3300
—and—
1139 Magnolia • Larkspur, CA 94939 • 415-461-0351

Pat and Stan Painter began with The Painters Place in 1966 in Larkspur. In 1978, they opened a second shop on Hayes Street in San Francisco. Now owned and operated by sons Matt and Tom, the business has a third location in Berkeley. Their philosophy: "Every picture deserves a beautiful frame." They have executed work for Gumps, Macy's, Ralph Lauren Polo, as well as numerous art galleries and restaurants. They have perfected a number of unique and rare finishes using both oil and water gilding, they can "age" mirrors using an antique silvering process, and they will frame textiles, fans, medals and other three-dimensional objects. On-site consulting and installation services are also available.

ART, INSTALLATION

ARTWORKS

268 Bush Street #2725 • San Francisco, CA 94104
415-305-9869 • www.artworks415.com

After spending ten years in art gallery management, Juan Navarro II founded Artworks, which offers assistance to private or corporate clients in positioning, displaying, lighting, grouping and hanging techniques for art of all kinds, as well as photography and mirrors. He takes commissions all over the Bay Area, the Napa Valley and Lake Tahoe. By appointment.

MICHAEL GOARD
1269 Green Street • San Francisco, CA 94109
415-776-6935 • Michael@michaelgoard.com

From the moment you purchase your painting or sculpture, Michael will take care of all the details, including where to display it, and how to highlight it with natural or artificial lighting. In just one day, I watched Michael place a large heavy sculpture in a garden, hang an Old Master painting in a home, and (the piece-de-resistance) position a moose head over a fireplace.

HANG IT ALL
G.W. Frederick • 566 Pennsylvania Avenue
San Francisco, CA 94107 • 415-826-1052

G.W. (or Frederick—he goes by both names), a retired interior designer trained at the prestigious Parson's School of Design in New York, decided that a natural extension of his prior career would be the placement and hanging of art work. In San Francisco since 1980, G.W. will also advise clients as to where and how their collections should be displayed in relationship to their furnishings. He will work anywhere in the Bay Area. By appointment.

WILLIAM H. JONKE
415-771-3704

William Jonke's sterling reputation has come from executing superb residential and commercial art placement and installation commissions. William prefers to work in San Francsico, but on occasion will accept commissions around the Bay Area. By appointment.

ART, RENTAL

SAN FRANCISCO MOMA RENTAL GALLERY
Building A, Fort Mason Center • San Francisco, CA 94123
415-441-4777

An adjunct to the San Francisco Museum of Modern Art, the MOMA Rental Gallery leases and sells works by over 1,000 artists. Art lovers daunted by high price tags often find that renting a piece for as little as $15 a month is an economical alternative. After a few months, either return the work or buy it, with your rental fees credited towards the purchase price. This is an opportunity to hang great art on your walls while you learn about what you like to live with and what you don't.

ART, STORAGE

ATTHOWE FINE ART SERVICES
3924 Market Street • Oakland, CA 94608 • 510-654-6816

This third-generation business, founded in 1928, is dedicated to the safe handling of fine art and fragile objects. Services include transportation, packing, crating, installation and storage. With 80,000 square feet comprising climate-controlled storage vaults, woodworking shops, and secure packing and loading facilities. Atthowe's transport vehicles are also climate-controlled and traverse California and the Western states. The staff routinely works with museums, galleries, private collectors and artists to provide top quality personal service.

SHIP/ART INTERNATIONAL
P.O. Box 1176 • South San Francisco, CA 94083
650-952-0100 • www.shipart.com

Ship/Art International provides custom crating and packing of fine art for transportation, both domestic and international, as well as 50,000 square feet of monitored storage space, with

20,000 square feet that is temperature controlled. Backed by more than twenty years of experience in the field, Ship/Art has a complete line of archival wrapping and packing products insuring that your art is preserved to the highest museum standards.

ARTISTIC RENDERINGS

JUDY MCBRIDE
1738 Stanley Dollar Drive #2B • Walnut Creek, CA 94595
925-935-9700

Since her retirement from The Wiseman Group, a prestigious San Francisco design firm, Judy has pursued her love of illustrated room renderings and has become a tour de force in this field. Whether you desire an interior rendering for your personal collection or for conceptual use during design and construction, Judy is happy to work anywhere in the Bay Area. By appointment.

JULIE LEVIN
128 Coronado Street • El Granada, CA 94018
650-712-9321 • julielyn20031@yahoo.com

A graduate from San Francisco State University from their interior design program, Julie is a multi-talented artist who does drafting, perspective drawings, interior design renderings in pen, marker, pencil, charcoal, pencil, and ink and will do both interior and exterior renderings. Julie will even include the family pet sitting on the living room sofa! By appointment.

BATHROOM TILE RESTORATION

MR. BATHTUB, INC.
1-800-672-2848 • www.mrbathtub.com

Mr. Bathtub does it all! Including re-coloring and re-grouting your old tile, changing the color on that old tub and sink, refinishing the shower, repairing unsightly cracks in the plaster, etc. In business since 1980, the hard-working folks at Mr. Bathtub give a five-year guarantee for their work in seven counties: San Francisco, Contra Costa, Marin, Alameda, Santa Cruz, San Mateo and Santa Clara.

MIRACLE METHOD SURFACE RESTORATION
1-888-271-7690

Call for a referral in your area, as this is a franchise with seven different companies providing service throughout the Bay Area. In business since 1978, Miracle Method will come to your house and give a free estimate to recolor your old tile in a bonded enamel finish. Miracle Method also does porcelain re-glazing, tub resurfacing and restoration of similar surfaces (sinks, commodes, etc.) to a brand-new condition. Damaged, stained or worn fiberglass can also be restored.

THE GROUT DOCTOR OF OAKLAND
510-530-3104

Give Charles Pellicci a call for a free estimate when your grout needs a good cleaning and/or replacing. He can also re-color your grout if thorough cleaning and sealing don't do the job for you.

In business since 1993, The Grout Doctor will make house calls throughout the Bay Area. Note that cleaning and replacing grout is all they do—sorry, no tile replacement.

BED LINENS, CUSTOM

ANGELIQUE'S INTERIORS
(See Windows, Curtains & Draperies)

DREAMS
(See Pillow & Cushion Fabrication)

SUE FISHER KING
3067 Sacramento Street • San Francisco, CA 94115
415-922-7276

Open since 1979, Sue provides luxury bed and table linens and has expanded to include fine bed linens custom-sized to fit the bedding needs of her clients' yachts and jets as well as their homes. Sue Fisher King also offers a line of lamps and lighting to color coordinate with her linens as well as special to-order glazes for an exclusive line of pottery.

BOOK, AUCTION

PACIFIC BOOK AUCTION GALLERIES
133 Kearny Street, 4th Floor • San Francisco, CA 94108
415-989-2665 • www.pbagalleries.com

Devoted to works on paper, PBA conducts approximately twenty-five gallery auctions per calendar year and holds continuous live auctions of rare books, manuscripts, autographs, letters, documents, maps, atlases, prints and photographs. Whether you're de-accessioning or adding to your collection, attending an auction is a learning experience that's always fun. If you're selling, ask for George Fox.

BOOK, BINDING & REPAIR

PETTINGELL BOOK BINDERY
2181 Bancroft Way • Berkeley, CA 94704 • 510-845-3653

Klaus-Ullrich Rotzscher has worked as a bookbinder par excellence since 1975. He gives each labor-intensive job the same painstakingly personal attention. When restoring an antique book, Klaus makes every effort to reassemble it using its own materials. Only if it is totally irrepairable will he craft replacement parts from new materials carefully fashioned to appear as old as the original. Klaus also creates handsome new bindings using quality linen, leather or paper, gold stamping and stunning marbled endpapers. Klaus once told me that he feels his work is not only a labor of love, it is love of the labor.

SPIRAL BINDING
2730 16th Street • San Francisco, CA 94103 • 415-864-6330

One of a handful of binderies left in San Francisco, this one is owned and operated by Doug MacNeil, who took over from his father in the early 1990s. In addition to books, Spiral Binding binds reports, brochures, architectural plans—you name it, they'll bind it. They also do intricate folding jobs for pamphlets, brochures, and other paper materials.

TAURUS BOOKBINDERY
Tim James • 1555 Yosemite Avenue #16
San Francisco, CA 94124 • 415-671-2233
www.taurusbookbindery.com
—and—
Scott Newel
2748 Ninth Street • Berkeley, CA 94710 • 510-548-2313

At Taurus, they'll ask you to start with the presumption that it will undoubtedly be less expensive to purchase a new book than it will be to repair the old one. That said, nearly any book can be repaired, and if it has sentimental value then it is truly worth the price. In business since 1990, Taurus makes new books, portfolios, presentation folders, family histories, pamphlets, etc.

BOOK, FABRICATION

NICOLE ANDERSON
3260 Wyman Street • Oakland, CA 94619 • 510-533-0333

Nicole Anderson's goal is to produce the highest quality hand-made albums, portfolios, guest books, and boxes, using the finest materials available. She thrives on challenges and happily will tackle the odd-shaped book or an unusual request for materials or colors. All work is done on acid-free paper to insure that your special treasure will last forever. Nicole will also create a slipcase for your treasured book, either for storage or presentation.

PETTINGELL BOOK BINDERY
(See Book, Binding & Repair)

BOOKS, USED

SAN FRANCISCO PUBLIC LIBRARY, MAIN BRANCH

100 Larkin Street • San Francisco, CA 94102 • 415-557-4400

Are you looking to fill up those empty bookcases? The Friends of the San Francisco Public Library's annual September used-book sale is an event Bay Area book lovers always look forward to. But the real bargains are at the mini-sales held every month (weather permitting) on the steps of the main branch and four times a year in an annex at Fort Mason Center, Building C. Each mini-sale features thousands of books.

BOOK SHELF ORGANIZER/ADVISOR

VICTORIA BAYLON

945 Pine Street #7 • San Francisco, CA 94108
415-351-2580 • victoriab2001@yahoo.com

Known as the "book stylist," Victoria organizes and arranges bookcases by creating a visually appealing display with an artful mix of her client's collectables and personal library. Since Victoria is an avid book collector herself, she also provides a search service for those wishing to add to their collections. She charges by the hour but the initial in-home consultation is free.

BRASS, COPPER, SILVER CLEANING, PLATING & RESTORATION

BIRO & SONS SILVERSMITHS

1160 Folsom Street • San Francisco, CA 94103
415-431-3480 • www.biroandsons.com

Family-owned and operated since 1945, Biro & Sons design and manufacture their own line of fine sterling and silverplated hollowware. They employ a creative staff that is able to provide custom, individual metal-crafting on site and offer antique restoration services guaranteed to return the luster to your treasured family heirlooms.

J & A POLISHING

2635 Land Avenue • Sacramento, CA 95815 • 916-922-0300
—and—
1347 Donner Street • San Francisco CA 94124 • 415-822-2260

After twenty years of operation in San Francisco, Joe and Arsenio moved the company to Sacramento. To keep their Bay Area clients happy, they maintain an office at the Donner Street address where you may drop off your items on Mondays between 8 and 3:30. Joe takes them to Sacramento and returns them cleaned the following Monday. They handle nearly all metals, including silver, copper, brass, aluminum, and stainless steel. Also, they will refinish brass on request, giving shiny new pieces an antique patina or vice versa.

MONSEN PLATING & SILVERSMITHS

3370 Adeline Street • Berkeley, CA 94703
510-655-0890 • www.monsenplating.com

Established in 1904, Monsen's master craftsmen have been working in silver, gold, copper, nickel, brass, bronze, pewter and other alloys for over a century. They can replicate missing parts, remove dents and dings, buff out scratches, re-solder old repairs and re-plate virtually anything. If you inherited great Grandma's silver hairbrush and mirror set, they'll not only refurbish the silver, they'll add new bristles to the brush and replace the mirror that you can no longer see yourself in. If your flatware (be it sterling or plate) gets mangled in the garbage disposal, they will straighten and repair it.

PILGRAM PLATING

757 Lincoln, Suite 24 • San Rafael, CA 94901
415-456-1525

Kim Colla's services have been in demand since the mid-1980s by interior decorators, antiques dealers and building contractors. He specializes in cleaning, plating, repairing and refinishing antique brass, silver, copper and nickel. He'll tackle all home interior hardware including bathroom, kitchen and light fixtures. Kim can match any finish, whether it's a mellow 19th century patina or a sleek 21st century shine.

C

CANDLES

FANTASTICO
559 Sixth Street • San Francisco, CA 94103
415-982-0680

This warehouse is chock full of decorative home accessories, including dried flowers, paper goods and baskets. But what I shop for are the candles. The wonderful selection of sizes and colors make them a bargain by the boxful. Many designers I know consider Fantastico's a "trade only" secret source, but they're open to the public for everyone to enjoy!

CARPET & AREA RUG CLEANING

BURROUS BROTHERS COMPANY
98 Main Street • Tiburon, CA 94920
415-435-1588 • www.bbc-cleaning.com

Frank Burrous began cleaning rugs and upholstery in 1976. He recently added stone, tile and grout cleaning to the company's services. Year after year, Burrous Brothers receives the highest ratings from the Bay Area Consumers Checkbook, a non-profit consumer watchdog group. Unfortunately for the rest of us, they work exclusively in Marin County.

GROMM RUG & UPHOLSTERY CLEANING
370 Fourth Street • Montara, CA • 650-728-5666

Frank Gromm is the third generation in his family in the rug and upholstery cleaning business. He schedules appointments all over the Bay Area and is in the City nearly every day. Frank will tackle every imaginable stain and dirt problem on most fabrics and textiles, including wool, nylon, silk, and Oriental rugs. All work is done on site in the client's home. By appointment.

CARPET INSTALLATION

DAN YU CARPET CO.
780 Florida Street • San Francisco, CA 94110 • 415-664-1810

Thinking about purchasing new carpeting for your home or office? Step one is to give Dan Yu a call. Anna will probably answer the phone, so make an appointment with her for Dan to come out to measure the site and estimate yardage requirements and installation costs. After you order your new carpeting, have it delivered to Dan's loading dock on Florida Street, and then relax. Dan works all over the Bay Area by appointment.

JERRY PROVERT
415-641-5657

Jerry has done residential and commercial carpet installation since the late 1970s and works mainly in San Francisco, where he maintains a warehouse. Jerry does everything himself, and although he prefers working Monday through Friday, if your installation requires the weekend to complete, you can absolutely depend on Jerry to show up and finish the job. By appointment.

CARPET REPAIR

GARY MEYERS CARPET REPAIR
415-456-3834

Gary Meyers started his "new" business by accident when, after forty years in the carpet business, he started helping out his carpet dealer colleagues by doing repairs for their clients. Today, he tackles holes, tears, burns, bleach spots, and water damage. Gary uses

C

time-tested repair techniques that many carpet installers don't even know about. He works in Marin County, southern Sonoma County and San Francisco by appointment.

CATERING

BARBARA LLEWELLYN
100 Overhill Road • Orinda, CA 94563
510-832-1967 • www.barbarallewellyn.com

In business since 1990, Barbara is known for her relaxed style, individualized menus, the creative use of the venue whether it's an intimate dinner for eight or a cocktail bash for a thousand. And for hostesses with no time to plan or cook but wish to look like they did, she also offers a delivery and pick-up service for in-home parties. How great is that? Barbara works throughout the Bay Area, Lake Tahoe, the Napa Valley and Monterey County.

BETTY ZLATCHIN CATERING
1177 Indiana Street • San Francisco, CA 94107
415-641-8599 • info@bettyzlatchin.com

Betty's focus has always been high quality, and her staff, headed by chef Tom, formerly at Zuni Café, and sous chef Sophina Uong, does truly exceptional food presentation. Betty's son David joined the company in 2001 after earning his Master's degree in business from UC Berkeley. Betty and her staff travel as frequently as possible to France and the Mediterranean for ongoing inspiration, which they feel is as important to their business as using the freshest and finest seasonal ingredients available.

HEIDI BOTTOM
415-377-6838 • heidi_bottom@yahoo.com

After attending Tante Marie's Cooking School in San Francisco. Heidi continued her studies abroad before returning to the Bay Area in 2003 to open her own catering business. One of Heidi's unique entertaining options is a dinner party/cooking class in your home. She plans the menu, brings the ingredients, and does the prep work. Once your guests arrive, they prepare each course with Heidi's expert supervision. While you and your guests enjoy the meal, Heidi cleans up the kitchen.

MCCALL ASSOCIATES

350 Florida Street • San Francisco, CA 94110
415-552-8550 • mccall@danmccall.com

A former director of catering for the St. Francis Hotel, Dan McCall founded his own firm back in 1980. Today, it reigns as one of the premier catering companies in the Bay Area. Not limited to menu planning and food preparation and presentation, McCall Associates will orchestrate your entire event, including table décor, floral arrangements, and lighting. They handle over eight hundred events every year.

JANE HAMMOND EVENTS, INC.

1975 Yosemite Road • Berkeley, CA 94707
510-528-3530 • jane@jhevents.com

Jane Hammond Events has been providing full service catering for corporate and large private events throughout the San Francisco Bay Area since 1980. Because they're from Berkeley, the birthplace of California Cuisine, one of their hallmarks is using the freshest ingredients available in creative combinations.

OUT OF THYME CATERING

2470 Fifteenth Street, Suite 4 • San Francisco, CA 94114
415-252-9110

Doug Skonie, chef de cuisine, and Dave Haase, event designer, were friends for ten years before joining forces in 2003 when they were inspired to open their own catering and event-planning business. If you're planning an intimate luncheon, a holiday dinner party, or a major community event, it will all be accomplished in their seamless and stress-free style and, most important, within your budget constraints.

PAULA LE DUC FINE CATERING

1350 Park Avenue • Emeryville, CA 94608 • 510-547-7825

Paula Le Duc's motto is "Perfect will be just fine" and she never fails to deliver exactly that. Since 1984, Paula Le Duc has been ranked consistently as one of the top Bay Area caterers. Presentations are visually stunning and the food is unsurpassed in flavor and quality. The secret is attention to even the most minute detail. Prices are not for the faint-hearted, but if your budget can take it, they're worth every cent.

PRIVATE AFFAIRS

1833-A McAllister Street • San Francisco, CA 94115
415-673-9329 • 415-218-4131 (cell)

David Bowers and Bruce Ivie prefer to work on more intimate gatherings in private home rather than large events in more public or less personal venues. Whether they're creating a romantic Valentine's dinner for two or a festive cocktail party for two hundred, David and Bruce will plan it, prepare it, serve it, and clean up afterwards. Sounds ideal to me!

SUSAN MOSELEY

19 Landers Street • San Francisco, CA 94114
415-282-6976 • suzyqsf@yahoo.com

Susan has always been innovative with her menus while being sensitive to her client's dietary restrictions and/or requests. In recent years, she has focused primarily on one facet of the business—producing memorable cocktail parties of any size with a scrumptious repertoire of hors d'oeuvres and snacks. She will also act as a temporary personal assistant/project manager for clients who need help putting together large events and celebrations.

CHANDELIER CLEANING

FOX CHANDELIER CLEANING
Rebecca Fox
415-682-7511 • www.foxchandeliercleaning.com

I would describe Rebecca's work as chandelier detailing because she is such a perfectionist. Rebecca will not only clean any type of hanging chandelier, including the most intricate and delicate Italian Murano glass fixtures, but also wall sconces and lanterns, both interior and exterior. All work is done on site in your home. By appointment only.

HANG IT ALL
(See Art, Installation)

CHINA & CRYSTAL REPLACEMENT

HERITAGE HOUSE, INC.
2190 Palou Avenue • San Francisco, CA 94124
415-285-1331 • 1-800-776-6873
www.heritagehouse.net

Heritage House, Inc. is a bridal registry and showroom in business since 1963 with over 1,800 patterns of fine china, crystal, and flatware at discounted prices with savings ranging from 10% to 50% off manufacturers' retail prices. In addition to a knowledgable staff, Heritage House offers buyers the opportunity to try sample place settings at home on approval. They have a replacement service as well as a sterling pattern matching service. Open Monday though Friday 10 to 6 and Saturday 10 to 5.

REPLACEMENTS, LTD.

1089 Knox Road • P.O. Box 26029 • Greensboro, NC 27420
1-800-737-5223 • www.replacements.com
inquire@replacements.com

Stocking over 10,000,000 (that's ten million) pieces of china in more than 20,000 patterns on more than 60,000 shelves in their warehouse, Replacements has a staff of 500 people and a rotating "staff" of 15 to 25 pets. (Customers are encouraged to bring in their well-mannered animals as well.) Founded by Bob Page in 1981, Replacements offers the world's largest selection of old and new dinnerware, glassware and silver. If you need a piece to fill out your set, send them an email with the pertinent information and their matching service will supply a list of available replacements. They stock patterns dating back to the mid-1700s! They also offer a free pattern ID service. Just send a photo of the front and back of your item and they will identify it for you.

CLOCK & WATCH REPAIR

CLOCKWORLD

1512 Pine Street • San Francisco, CA 94109
415-346-0228

Clockworld handles antique and new clocks, and watches. They give a free estimate, will make a service call to your home, offer competitive prices and all their work is guaranteed. Open Monday through Saturday 10 to 6.

DORIAN CLAIR

1301 Sanchez • San Francisco, CA 94131 • 415-648-8680

In addition to being known for expert clock repair and restoration work, Dorian Clair's customers also drop by to renew their acquaintance with Taffy, the big yellow cat who lives in the front window of the shop. With over five decades worth of experience, Dorian was a natural to be chosen to maintain the Ferry Building clock in San Francisco and the Memorial Church tower on the Stanford University campus. In fact, he works on most of the tower clocks in the Bay Area. Dorian is usually in the shop 9:30 to 4:30 Monday through Friday and 9:30 to 4 on Saturday.

SMITH CLOCK CO.
2799 Bush Street • San Francisco, CA 94115 • 415-921-1267

With more than thirty years of experience under his belt, David Smith works on all types of timepieces, but primarily on American, German, French, Dutch or Austrian clocks. Many antique dealers employ his services because he can reproduce missing or damaged pieces from old mechanisms. He also specializes in assisting homeowners with clock re-location—many clocks require careful disassembly prior to packing, followed by reassembly after the move. Wednesday through Saturday 11 to 5, Monday and Tuesday by appointment.

WALTER LOELIGER
50 Flight Road • Carmel Valley Village, CA 93924 • 831-659-8646

Walter Loeliger has been plying his craft with traditional European workmanship since 1971—and I've been using him that long! Although all work is done in his Carmel Valley workshop, Walter drives to the Bay Area every two weeks for pick-up and delivery among his faithful customers. In addition to expert clock restoration, Walter also works on music boxes, barometers, and a variety of scientific instruments and is often called upon to repair items made from famously finicky materials such as tole, pewter, ivory, and tortoiseshell.

WASHINGTON CLOCK COMPANY
1130 Harrison • San Francisco, CA 94103 • 415-864-2456

In business for nearly sixty years, forty-three of them in Pacific Heights, and now South of Market, Peter Weil and Jimmy Martin have formed a unique partnership. Jimmy, who turned ninety in 2005, purchased the business from its original owner and continued to manage it until 1999 when Peter purchased it with the loving stipulation that Jimmy may never retire. They stock old, rare, hard-to-find, even obsolete parts and movements, which means they can do repair and restoration jobs that others would pass on. You'll see many wonderful old clocks in their workshop and, if you're very lucky (and very persistent) you may convince them to sell one to you. Their dogs Rosie and Taddy make every visit to Peter and Jimmy's a pleasure.

COMPUTER SET UP & TRAINING

DREWKAI L. BUTLER
Drewkai@BAMSN.com • www.BAMSN.com • 415-713-8549

Drewkai teaches basic skills for beginners including how to use email and the Internet. For more advanced users, he provides trouble-shooting expertise, personal tutoring and training in formatting, spreadsheets, virus control, etc. He is skilled on PCs and Macs and has twenty years in the business. Drewkai's business is tailored for each individual user and the training is done at your own pace and in the privacy and comfort of your own home. By appointment.

J & M TECHNOLOGY SERVICES
Mike Barnes
6379 Camino Verde Dr. • San Jose, CA 95119 • 408-603-8848
mike.barnes@sbcglobal.net

Mike is a great guy. He has lots of personality as well as unlimited expertise in PC and Networking. He is a certified Microsoft Professional who will install your new computer and handle all the subsequent problems, including virus removal and disaster recovery when, god forbid, your computer crashes either at home or at the office. He also does server and printer maintenance. By appointment.

MARK PORIER
415-922-4357 • www.c-help.com

Mark is very patient and will tailor your training in your own home, on your own computer, at your own level. His range of technical and teaching skills allows him to solve problems, create solutions, and share his knowledge in a patient, friendly manner. He communicates new skills clearly and practices empathic listening skills that put his students and clients at ease. Mark has delivered software training in all skill levels for individuals, public classes and for private corporate groups. By appointment.

MILES CARNAHAN
125 Winfield Street • San Francisco, CA 94110
415-285-3862 • 415-350-3914 (cell) • miles_c@pacbell.net

Miles handled all of my computer problems during the writing of this book, and since I know nothing at all about cyber technology, he's been busy! In fact, there doesn't seem to be much that he cannot do to keep this machine of mine up and running. Miles is extremely patient and calm. He can teach the most basic computer skills to a beginner as well as assist an advanced user with technology problems. By appointment.

CONSIGNMENT SERVICE, CLOTHING

CHRIS CONSIGNMENT
2056 Polk Street • San Francisco, CA 94109 • 415-474-1191

Chris Consignment offers the crème de la crème of consigned clothing and accessories. A delicious secret among style-conscious but budget-minded San Francisco shoppers, Chris carries top couture labels like Marc Jacobs, Prada, and Gucci, as well as more cutting-edge designer labels like Voyage and ChloZ. They stock both men's and women's fashions. Monday through Friday 11 to 6:30, Saturday 11 to 6, and Sunday 11 to 5.

DESIGNER CONSIGNER

3464 Sacramento Street • San Francisco, CA 94118 • 415-440-8664

Looking for high style at low prices? Then you'll love a consignment shop that attracts high-end designer and couture clothing. Bay Area fashionistas love the selections from Chanel, Gucci, Versace, and Hermes. Take some of your own pieces in with you (in good condition, of course) and you may receive a 40% discount off your purchase. I took a Chanel suit in to re-sell and was happily surprised when, a few weeks later, I received a surprisingly large check in the mail. Women's clothing only. Open every day, Monday through Saturday 10 to 6, Sunday 11 to 5.

GOOD BYES

3464 Sacramento Street • San Francisco, CA 94118
415-346-6388

There are two Good Byes consignment shops—one carrying men's designer clothing and one with women's clothing right across the street. Good Byes carry not just the couture heavy-weights like Armani, Versace, Chanel, St. John, but also J. Crew, Banana Republic and Ann Taylor. They designate certain days of the week at each store to purchase clothing in good condition, so call ahead if you're in the mood to clean out your closet. Hours are Monday, Wednesday, Friday and Saturday 10 to 6, Thursday 10 to 8 and Sunday 11 to 5.

KIMBERLEY'S CONSIGNMENT COUTURE

3020 Clement Street • San Francisco, CA 94121
415-752-2223

Kimberley's carries designer clothing for men and women for a fraction of the retail price, Gucci, Versace, DKNY, Prada and more. This store adheres to highly selective criteria when choosing its re-sale garments: each item must be less than three years old and in mint condition. Consignments are accepted daily. Hours are 11 to 5 Tuesday through Saturday and 11 to 3 on the first Sunday of the month.

CONSIGNMENT SERVICE, FURNITURE

CONSIGNMENT SHOWCASE

57 Town & Country Village • Palo Alto, CA 94301

650-463-5950

Consignment Showcase features outstanding bargains on high-end, high-quality home furnishings, accessories, art and flatware. All merchandise comes from private homes and estates. Not only is this a fun place to shop, it's a great venue when you're ready to recycle your own furniture and decorative items. The prices are quite reasonable and the items taken for re-sale in excellent condition and offer great value. Their hours are Monday through Friday 10 to 6, Saturday 10 to 5 and Sunday noon to 5.

RICOCHET CONSIGNMENT

4062 Watts Street • Emeryville, CA 94608

510-923-1422 • www.ricochetconsignment.homestead.com

Their logo is "furniture with experience" and their 9,000-square-foot location offers an eclectic mix of furniture, antiques, accessories, lighting fixtures and unique decorative objects. Inventory comes from estate sales, interior designers' showrooms as well as Bay Area homeowners. If you're in the market to sell rather than buy, it's a good idea to take photos of your items by their location first. Ricochet accepts consignments on a two-month basis at a very fair 50% split with the consignee.

D

DELIVERY & MOVING

BORG TRUCKING
100 Robinson Drive • San Francisco, CA 94112
415-334-3241 • 415-215-3864 (cell)
borgtrucking@netscape.net

With more than twenty years experience behind him, George Borg started his business to facilitate local deliveries for interior designers and their clients. Although he does not provide shipping and receiving services, George is quite flexible with his time and does everything he can to be accommodating. The best way to reach him is on his cell phone.

CARLSON VAN LINES
306 Littlefield • South San Francisco, CA 94080 • 1-800-892-9201

Carlson Van Lines drives weekly between the Bay Area and L.A., with stops en route by prior arrangement, generally picking up in San Francisco on Tuesday or Thursday and delivering in Los Angeles by the end of the week. A day or so later, they do a turn around. I have used them for years and they continue to offer the same reliable service. Ask for Bill, Eric or Lou Ann.

DESIGNER'S DELIVERY
1401 Franquette • Concord, CA 94520 • 925-671-7694

George Cabral and his wife have owned this East Bay delivery service since 1978. They do blanket-wrap local delivery from San Jose and Los Gatos, to San Francisco, the Wine Country and all over the East Bay. Designer's Delivery also does household moving and will provide short-term storage when necessary on request. They do no crating or packing. Monday through Friday 7 to 4.

ELWELL TRUCKING

1420 Carroll Avenue • San Francisco, CA 94124 • 415-822-5500

Elwell Trucking offers extremely reliable moving and storage service for the Bay Area. They will move just about anything and store it for as little as a few days or as long as several months. Ask for Raul or Bob when planning your next move.

KILLIAN'S FINE FURNITURE DELIVERY

1039 Cedar Street • Berkeley, CA 94710 • 415-971-3371

Killian Macgeraghty offers a local pick-up and delivery service that's actually unique: when you schedule your pick-up or delivery with him, he will assign you a one-hour window to be home and then he gets there within that time! So if you don't have half a day to wait for a delivery truck, give Killian a try.

NOE'S FURNITURE DELIVERY

P. O. Box 410895 • San Francisco, CA 94141 • 415-652-0175

Noe Leon specializes in moving fragile and costly antiques, has extremely fair rates, and will provide references on request. Noe and his assistant prefer smaller moving jobs, they work quickly and efficiently, and are often available for last minute deliveries.

DRY CLEANING—EXTRA CARE

G. F. THOMAS

859 14th Street • San Francisco, CA 94114 • 415-861-0969

Emile Thomas is the fourth-generation owner of this specialty care cleaners, founded in 1854 and in its present location since 1906. Thomas's will clean delicate apparel and vintage wedding gowns and prepare them for long-time storage. Mr. Thomas will make house calls to assess other cleaning requests such as furniture and draperies. Open Monday through Friday 7:30 to 6 and Saturday 7:30 to 1.

HOLIDAY CLEANERS

1820 Polk Street • San Francisco, CA 94109 • 415-928-5707

Vanessa Chin has owned and operated this service-oriented dry cleaning establishment for nearly twenty years and offers specialty care for labor-intensive table and bed linens. Pressing and cleaning are all done in-house. Vanessa does no advertising—her reputation for quality workmanship has spread only by word of mouth. Regular customers who live in the neighborhood can ask Vanessa to pick-up and deliver to your home. Closed Sunday and Monday.

PENINOU FRENCH LAUNDRY & CLEANERS

3707 Sacramento Street • San Francisco, CA 94118
415-751-7050
 —and—
3063 Laguna Street • San Francisco, CA 94104 • 415-351-2554
 —and—
558 Oak Grove Avenue • Menlo Park, CA 94025 • 650-322-7562

In business for over 100 years, Peninou is a family-run operation founded in 1903 that today spans three generations, all currently working together. Peninou has received numerous local and national business and consumer awards. They specialize in museum-quality restoration and preservation of wedding gowns and table linens. They offer complimentary pick-up and delivery services in San Francisco, Marin County, and on the Peninsula. Hours are 7 to 6:30 Monday through Friday and 9 to 5 on Saturday.

E

ELECTRICIAN

KINETIC ELECTRIC
567 Anderson Street • San Francisco, CA 94110
415-517-4919 • kineticelectric@earthlink.net

Isabella Battig is a rarity: she is one of the very few licensed female electricians in the Bay Area. Isabella, who owns her company, usually works alone, but will bring an assistant if she feels the job warrants it. She accepts jobs all over San Francisco, the East Bay and Marin County and is happy to take on smaller projects that other electricians might pass on (installing a light fixture) but is equally comfortable working with contractors on large projects (home or business remodel).

ESTATE AUCTION HOUSES

BONHAMS & BUTTERFIELDS
220 San Bruno Avenue • San Francisco, CA 94103
415-861-7500 • www.bonhams.com/us

Founded in 1865, the venerable Butterfields was acquired by Bonhams in 2002, making Bonhams & Butterfields the third largest auction house in the world, with houses in San Francisco and Los Angeles, and regional offices in Arizona, Illinois, Nevada, New York, Oregon, Washington and Canada. In addition to estate auctions, they also offer free appraisal days on a monthly basis.

SAN RAFAEL AUCTION GALLERY

634 Fifth Avenue • San Rafael, CA 94901

415-457-4488 • www.sanrafaelauction@aol.com

The San Rafael Auction Gallery has been auctioning antiques, paintings, and decorative arts for more than twenty years. There is no charge to bid, however you must complete a registration form in order to do so. Auctions are held on Saturday at 10 A.M. and you may preview the items from Friday noon until 8 P.M. and Saturday 8 to 10 A.M. Call during the week if you have items to consign.

ESTATE LIQUIDATOR

JOHN FAVORS ESTATE LIQUIDATORS

700 26th Street • Oakland, CA 94611

510-663-0449

John Favors has been in the business since 1980, serving the Bay Area and beyond where he does approximately 250 liquidations a year. Some liquidations simply require that a property be cleared so it can be sold. Others may require an on-site sale, or an off-site warehouse sale. John handles household personal property of virtually any value, including cars, jewelry, rugs, paintings and furniture.

FABRIC, ANTIQUE & RARE

LOTUS COLLECTION
445 Jackson Street • San Francisco, CA 94111
415-398-8115 • www.ktaylor-lotus.com

The Lotus Collection is a preeminent resource for buying and selling antique and unusual textiles. Kathleen Taylor regularly travels the country—and the world—in search of fine and rare Asian and European fabrics and tapestries. Open Monday through Friday 10 to 5 and Saturday 11 to 4.

FABRIC FINISHING & PROTECTION

GELTMAN INDUSTRIES
1901 Sacramento Street • Los Angeles, CA 90021
213-622-2015

Do you have a bolt of fabric that needs to be pre-shrunk before it's made into custom slipcovers? How about a protective laminate on your wrought-iron garden furniture? Need a fabric backing (imperative if you're using delicate material)? If your answer is yes to any of these questions, then you need Geltmans, also known as "the fabric finishers." Monday through Friday 7:30 to 5. Ask for Mark in customer service.

PRO-TECTION
Dan Coakley • 415-861-2300

Referred by top interior decorators, Dan offers two simple, but potentially invaluable in-home procedures. The first is a non-toxic substance sprayed directly onto upholstered furniture (it does no harm to wood or metal) that protects the fabric from organic soils and stains. The second is a mylar film applied directly to glass windowpanes that protects interior furnishings from the damaging effects of direct sunlight and UV infiltration. Each product can potentially more than double the life of your synthetic or natural fabrics. Work is done on-site, by appointment, and on a referral basis. (Dan does no advertising.) Call for a consultation.

FABRIC, RETAIL

BOCA BARGOON
24780 Hesperian Blvd. • Hayward, CA 94545 • 510-783-0323

Boca Bargoon is a high-end fabric outlet that stocks upholstery suedes, linens, velvets, brocades, liseres, denims, embroideries, chintzes, moirés, damasks, silks, and more from famous manufacturers like Scalamandre, Brunschwig & Fils, Ralph Lauren, Pierre Frey, Kravet and Robert Allen. They also carry a huge inventory of trims, tassels, gimps, welting, beading and fringe. Their outlet prices are hard to beat. And if they run out of an item, they'll re-order it and guarantee the original low price. Open Monday through Saturday 10 to 6.

BRITEX
146 Geary Street • San Francisco, CA 94108 • 415-392-2910

In business since 1952, Britex is a San Francisco institution. Approximately 12,000 square feet of retail space on four floors is crammed to the rafters with dress, upholstery and home decorating fabrics, sewing notions, accessories, and trims. They also stock a large section of remnants and bolt ends at impressive price reductions. Open Monday through Saturday 9:30 to 6, until 7 on Thursdays.

DHARMA TRADING CO.

1604 Fourth Street • San Rafael, CA 94901 • 415-456-1211

This unusual shop stocks domestic and imported yarns for knitting and weaving, as well as embroidery thread, beading, tie-dye paints and white clothing and fabrics that are ready to be dyed and decorated. There is a room (particularly interesting to designers) stocked only with white fabrics—silk, sateen, damask, cotton, fringe, cording and ribbon—all custom dye-able. Dharma Trading also offers very popular classes in knitting and crochet. Open 10 to 6 Monday through Saturday.

FRANK'S LEATHER & HIDES

3007 17th Street • San Francisco, CA • 415-551-1405

In business since 1857, this San Francisco landmark is a favorite with decorators and architects. Frank's inventory comes exclusively from domestic animals, such as cowhide and sheepskin—no trapped or exotic skins are stocked. Instead, Frank's carries a line of simulated exotics (for instance, cowhide stenciled to look like zebra skin or embossed to imitate crocodile or ostrich). The showroom is open from 8 to 4 Monday through Friday, although they prefer to see customers before 11:30. They also provide a matching service by mail. Send a swatch of the color and type of hide you're looking for and they'll do their best to hunt it down.

POPPY FABRIC

5151 Broadway • Oakland, CA 94611 • 510-655-5151

In business since 1975, Poppy carries bolt ends from manufacturers producing fabric for Perry Ellis, Prada, and other great designer names, in addition to a dazzling range of silks from Thailand, pretty Provençal cottons from France (a Poppy signature fabric), beaded gauze from India, as well as cozy fleece, flannel, and faux fur. A unique feature of Poppy's is their Custom Labor & Design Services department, headed by the vivacious Patti Popovich. Patti acts as a liaison between customer and the custom workrooms (offering upholstery, window treatment, and bedding design services). You'll need an appointment for a consultation. Open Monday through Friday 10 to 7, Saturday 10 to 5 and Sunday 12 to 5.

NORMAN S. BERNIE CO.

1135 No. Amphlett Blvd. • San Mateo, CA 94401
650-342-8586

Norman Bernie Company, a fixture in the fabric business for more than thirty-five years, passed from father to son in 1990. Cliff Bernie continues to offer fabrics at retail that would normally only be available "to the trade" in a designer showroom. Purchase a few yards or the whole bolt. You can even try a bolt at home for a few days on approval. Ask for Martha. Open Monday through Friday 10 to 5:30 and the first Saturday of every month 10 to 2.

SAL BERESSI FABRICS

1504 Bryant • San Francisco, CA 94103 • 415-861-5004

In 2005, after more than fifty years in the business and nearing his ninetieth birthday, Sal sold the company to Heather and John Kilpack. This dynamic couple is keeping up with trends while retaining Sal's competitive pricing. Their inventory includes famous names like Waverly, Schumacher and Robert Allen and is purchased directly from the mills. An interesting aside: while cleaning out an attic storeroom they found original bolts of material purchased during the 1950s, 60s and 70s. After being packed away for decades, these original vintage fabrics have made a comeback and the Kilpacks have created a "Retro Aisle" much to the delight of their customers. Tuesday through Saturday 10 to 6 .

THE RIBBONERIE INC.

191 Potrero Avenue • San Francisco, CA 94103
415-626-6184 • www.theribbonerie.com

The Ribbonerie opened its doors in 1997 and has been supplying the Bay Area with what I consider to be the most beautiful and unusual specialty ribbons on the West Coast. Paulette Knight and her mother Clara are in the shop each day from Tuesday through Friday 11 to 6 and Saturday 11 to 5. Much of their stock is exclusive to their shop. They feature a wonderful variety of French wired ribbons, as well as silk, velvet, jacquard, brocade, satin and grosgrain and a delightful assortment of passementerie, including metallic and beaded trims, tassels and fringes. Clara also collects and sells textile-related antiques and collectibles in the shop.

THE SILK TRADING CO.

1616A 16th Street • San Francisco, CA 94103
415-282-5574

In addition to the luxurious silk yardage they're known for, The Silk Trading Co. also stocks a lush interior organic-milk-based paint (similar to late eighteenth-century casein paints), as well as bedding and pillows, and a new line of drapery-out-of-a-box, created especially for customers in need of instant window treatment decorating solutions. Open Monday through Friday 10 to 6.

FABRIC RE-WEAVING

MENLO ATHERTON RE-WEAVERS

671 Oak Grove, Suite L • Menlo Park, CA 94025
650-322-0789

Teresa Kotsifakis and her associates Inocencia and Nina Smyrniotis have more than forty years of know-how between them and will tackle even the most challenging burns, tears, and holes in your favorite clothing. I was delighted when Teresa rescued a much-loved cashmere sweater (I thought it was beyond repair after catching the sleeve on a nail during a visit to a construction site). Open Monday through Friday 9 to 5:30 and Saturday 9 to 4:00.

FANTASY ARCHITECTURE & DESIGN

CREATIVE ARTS UNLIMITED

3730 70th Avenue No. • Pinellas Park, FL 33781
725-525-2066 • www.creativeartsinc.com

Do you have an outrageous idea for a room and a budget to make it happen? Creative Arts employs about thirty artisans in a 40,000-square-foot workshop who will conceptualize, build and install just about anything your imagination can conjure. Long known for sensational merchandising displays and museum installations (think Disneyland or Universal Studios) they are now fulfilling the dreams of private clients. You can expect to spend a minimum of $50,000, but what you'll get is totally over the top. Ask for President and Creative Director Roger Barganier when you call.

RAJ TENTS

6690 Pineneedle Drive • Oakland, CA 94611
510-654-4404 • infor@rajtents.com

In 2003, Dominic Mitchell and Maurice Walsh began importing fanciful tents to the West Coast for sale and rent after they became fascinated with the exotic examples Dominic's sister Clarissa discovered on a trip to Rajasthan and Jodhpur. Tents combine traditional craftsmanship and practical design with the inherent romance of these canopied portable pavilions and provide magical environments for weddings and all kinds of celebratory events.

TREEHOUSE WORKSHOP, INC.

2901 W. Commodore Way • Seattle, WA 98199
206-782-0208 • www.treehoseworkshop.com

Peter Nelson and Jake Jacob have been designing and building tree houses all over the world since 1998. Whether simple or splendid, a tree house makes a delightful guest suite, home office, craft studio, meditation pavilion, as well as a playroom for kids or getaway for grownups. Peter and Jake have teamed up with arborists and engineers to develop construction methods that reduce damage to the tree yet ensure a long life for the structure. These talented craftsmen use reclaimed and salvaged materials that give each house the appearance of having been in its tree forever. Visit their web site and let yourself dream.

FENG SHUI CONSULTING

MANU BUTTERWORTH

415-388-8166 • manu@seekingharmony.com

The founder and director of The Golden Gate School of Feng Shui is also a working feng shui consultant. He is available for private home as well corporate workplace consultations. Manu is also happy to advise architects, builders, realtors, and interior designers on large projects. By appointment.

DEBORAH GEE

1736 Stockton Street, Studio 9 • San Francisco, CA 94133
415-398-0292 • dgee@9star.net

Do you worry that a feng shui consultant will tell you to tear down a wall, move a door, or remodel your kitchen? Fear not! Deborah Gee will offer a simple, inexpensive design solution instead. Featured on PBS with her popular program "Feng Shui: Creating Environments for Success & Well-Being," she has consulted for Fortune 500 companies and now you can consult her too. San Francisco residents will be fascinated to learn that she consulted on the building of Pac Bell Park. By appointment.

FIREPLACE SURROUNDS & EQUIPMENT

OKELL'S FIREPLACE
1300 17th Street • San Francisco, CA 94102
415-626-1110 • www.okells.com

For decades, Okell's Fireplace has served the building and interior design trade exclusively. Now available to the public, they continue their fine tradition of producing some of the finest quality custom-made and one-of-a-kind fireplace equipment and accessories. Okell's also stocks antique fireplace surrounds, mantels, tools, and screens. Business hours are Monday through Friday 9 to 5 and Saturday 10 to 3.

FLOWERS, FRESH

WHOLESALE FLOWER MARKET
640 Brannon Street • San Francisco, CA 94103
415-392-7944 • www.sfflmart.com

Although most vendors at the Flower Mart prefer to sell exclusively wholsale, there are a few who will sell to retail customers provided there's no argument about paying sales tax. Also bear in mind it really isn't worth your time (or theirs) for one mixed bouquet. On the other hand, if you know what you want, and you know you need a lot of flowers (for a wedding or a company party) you can't beat the Flower Mart for variety. There are also a number of vendors selling ribbon and decorative trimmings, as well as floral arrangement foam, wire, moss, oasis, and other supplies that are not easy to find elsewhere. You'll pay retail but the selection is vast. Keep an eye on the time as most of the stalls and stores are closed by 11 A.M. but a few stay open later into the afternoon.

GARDEN VALLEY RANCH

498 Petaluma Road • Petaluma, CA 94952

707-795-0919

What began as a hobby in 1980 for Rosarian Ray Reddell is now a thriving business. Visitors are welcome to stroll the grounds Wednesday through Sunday for a very small fee, and a number of picturesque buildings dating back to the 1890s on the property are available for parties and weddings. The emphasis, however, is definitely on the roses! Shipping begins in April and there is a two-bunch (ten stems each) minimum order plus shipping. Last year Garden Valley Ranch shipped more than a quarter million roses around the country.

FURNITURE APPRAISAL

JOHN ANGUS MCKENZIE

(See Art, Appraisal)

LYON APPRAISAL

325M Sharon Park Drive #216 • Menlo Park, CA 94024

650-617-1065 • 415-288-4520 (San Francisco voicemail)

As a senior member of the American Society of Appraisers, Mary Kay Lyon does insurance and estate appraisals not only throughout the Bay Area, but also other locations by prior arrangement. By appointment.

FURNITURE, CUSTOM

DERAPAGE DESIGN
300 Kansas • San Francisco, CA 94103 • 415-552-9040
furniture@derapagedesign • www.derapage.com

Do you have a favorite corner cabinet but wish you had a matching piece for the other corner? Do you have a set of seven dining chairs and need eight? Mark Sommerfield has been making furniture since 1987 and can copy virtually any piece or create a custom design just for you. Mark also does thoughtful retrofitting of antiques to make them more functional as well as beautiful restoration work. This artisan of many talents is located near the Design Center. Open Monday through Friday 9 to 5.

J AND L REFINISHING CORP.
(See Furniture Refinishing, Restoration & Repair)

JOHN KENNAUGH
1717 Hyde Street • San Francisco, CA 94109 • 415-776-4223

John has been a one-man operation working out of a small, meticulously clean, well-organized workshop in the rear of his home since 1986 and, despite challenges (like scarce parking and the skyrocketing cost of living), he has beaten the odds and stayed in business. John is primarily a custom furniture maker who keeps his skills honed by hand-carving fireplace mantels and other architectural elements. Quality materials and refined joinery are features of his work. He also does residential on-site cabinetry and built-ins plus small repair jobs. By the way, he will pick up and deliver small items.

LUIS NORORI
(See Furniture Refinishing, Restoration & Repair)

ROSSI ANTIQUES
(See Furniture Refinishing, Restoration & Repair)

SAN FRANCISCO CUSTOM FURNITURE

Pier 5, Shed B #21 • San Francisco, CA 94107

415-243-4101

Located in the shadow of SBC Park, Kuldip Singh Sian creates handmade one-of-a-kind future heirlooms. His pieces are usually executed in fine woods, however he will also utilize exotic veneers and brass inlay. With only a drawing or photograph (even from a magazine or catalog) Kuldip can replicate a beautifully proportioned armoire, table, or chair. Call for an appointment.

THIS INTO THAT

2547 Eighth Street #30 • Berkeley, CA 94710

510-845-0106 • www.thisintothat.com

The grandson and son of publishing executives, Jim Rosenau grew up in a world devoted to books. Encouraging his passion for working with recycled wood, along with his devotion to old books, he has created a unique line of custom-built shelves and bookcases. The books come from donations, library sales, and recycling centers. No two bookcases or shelves are alike and express a different theme in each piece. Call him to discuss your ideas. Business hours can be irregular so it's a good idea to call for an appointment.

FURNITURE, DESIGNER SAMPLES

SAN FRANCISCO DESIGN CENTER

101 Henry Adams Street • San Francisco, CA 94103

415-490-5800 • www.sfdesigncenter.com

Twice a year the San Francisco Design Center hosts sample sales of furniture and accessories that are open to the public. The summer sale usually happens in May and the holiday sale during the Thanksgiving weekend, although dates are subject to change. Because the items on sale are showroom samples, they are sold in as-is condition and therefore priced at well below wholesale.

FURNITURE, IN-HOME REFINISHING, RESTORATION & REPAIR

KATIE MCCABE
(See Furniture Refinishing, Restoration & Repair)

QUALITY TOUCH
325 Ahwanee Lane • Clayton, CA 94517 • 925-673-8701

Bert Gomez had been working for Drexel Heritage Furniture for twenty years, when he saw the need for an in-home furniture detailing and restoration service. So in 2000, he started his own business doing what he likes to call "furniture facelifts" like buffing out scratches, regluing parts, and giving a professional polish to all the wood furniture in your home. He travels from Santa Rosa to Sacramento and Fresno as well as the Bay Area. Monday through Saturday by appointment.

FURNITURE, METAL

BLANK AND CABLES
950 63rd Street • Emeryville, CA 94608 • 415-648-3842

After graduation from the Rhode Island School of Design, Walter Craven moved west in 1995 where he has made quite a name for himself among architects and designers as one of the best custom metalworkers in the Bay Area. He does both residential and commercial work, and is known not only for finely crafted metal furniture, but also for innovative design in architectural elements, such as doors, gates, stairways and fireplace surrounds to name just a few. Walter works all over the Bay Area, and all over the world. Call or stop by Monday through Friday 7 to 3:30.

I OFF
1795 Bancroft • San Francisco, CA 94124 • 415-452-0456

Where did Mary Revelli get that name for her business? It's a term used for one-of-a-kind creations, and each piece Mary fabricates in her spacious workshop is unique. Described as the "welder with a design sense," she makes utilitarian furniture and fixtures as well as purely decorative pieces and is happy to partner with architects, decorators, contractors, and private individuals on large and smaller scale projects. She will copy antiques or work from original designs. By appointment 10 to 5, Monday through Friday.

FURNITURE, OUTDOOR FURNITURE RESTORATION

CLASSIC REFINISHING
125 Grobric Ct. #E • Fairfield, CA 94534
800-518-4888 • jcsclassic@earthlink.net

In business since 1989, this company reconditions aluminum, wrought or cast iron garden furniture. Whether it is re-strapping the webbing used under cushions or employing the latest technique for powder coating a new finish or determining and repairing structural damage to a frame, they will do it. Call for an estimate.

NEW DIMENSIONS
1755 Industrial Way #22 • Napa, CA 94558 • 707-255-7543

Peter and Linda Geyer started in 1985 doing seat and chair weaving. Out of this grew their quality restoration business specializing in outdoor metal furniture. Services include repairing, sandblasting, painting and powder coating, installing mesh slings, and weaving new vinyl strapping. They are factory-authorized to work on Brown Jordan furniture, including the older model bronze frames. They also work on other name brands, including Tropitone and Woodard, and will tackle outdoor umbrella repair. Linda also does caning, both hand and pressed, rush and rawhide seats, and wicker repair. Monday through Friday 9 to 12 and 1 to 5. Saturdays by appointment.

FURNITURE REFINISHING, RESTORATION & REPAIR

HECTOR DE LEON
1933 Davis Street #208 • San Leandro, CA 94577
510-639-7270 • 510-333-4783 (cell)

A favorite with local antique dealers, Hector has become one of the most respected furniture restorers in the Bay Area since he started in business in 1998. He takes great pride in doing the restoration work personally, which can make it challenging to book his time. In addition to exquisite refinishing, he can also take a piece that is literally in pieces and put it flawlessly back together. Hector prefers to pick-up and deliver all the furniture he works on. By appointment.

J AND L REFINISHING CORP.
820 Alabama Street • San Francisco, CA 94110 • 415-826-2505

In business since 1987, the artisans in this furniture restoration and conservation business not only restore and refinish older pieces, they are also highly regarded for their custom design and fabrication of new furniture as well. They can copy any piece of furniture, whether it is covered in ornate carving or has starkly simple lines. Ask to see their portfolio. Open Monday through Friday 8 to 5 and Saturday 10 to 3 or by appointment.

JAFE CUSTOM FINISHING
2425 17th Street • San Francisco, CA 94110 • 415-863-6196

Jeffery Mathieson has been providing custom wood refinishing in the Bay Area since 1970. He does on-site staining and refurbishing to wood paneling and cabinetry. So if your kitchen cupboards need just a touch-up or a total makeover with new stain color and a lustrous finish, Jeff and his staff can do it all. In addition, he will repair and refinish wood furniture at his 17th Street workroom. Jeff is also one of the few refinishers who repairs caned furniture. His restoration work for the McGuire Furniture showroom is an indication of his skill.

KATY MCCABE
1848 Sweetwood Drive • Colma, CA 94015
650-994-6367 • JMCS1622@aol.com

Katy McCabe has created a niche for herself by making house calls and providing personal service. On a home visit she will clean, touch-up and recolor surfaces where needed and wax your antique pieces with appropriately colored hard European waxes. She can take out water rings and other stains, and will make minor repairs to solid wood and veneers. More complicated jobs, such as regilding, are handled at her large workroom by a competent staff. By appointment Monday through Friday, 9 to 5.

LUIS NORORI
2250 Palou Avenue • San Francisco, CA 94124 • 415-206-9428

When Luis came to the U.S. in 1982, he swept floors and drove a delivery van for an antique shop just so he could learn the craft of furniture restoration. In 1993 he was ready to open his own business. Today he employs about a dozen talented craftsmen, including Cemil, a master wood carver from Turkey, and Joe, a gifted artist who can repair Chinoiserie lacquer work or virtually any painted finish. Their newest venture is a line of reproduction antique furniture, but Luis's first love will always be the preservation and restoration of genuine antique pieces. For a small fee they will pick-up and deliver. Hours are 8 to 4:30 Monday through Friday and 8 to 2 on Saturday.

MARIN FURNITURE CLINIC
(See Furniture, Wicker & Cane Repair)

RENAISSANCE FURNITURE RESTORATION

1600 Ocean Avenue • San Francisco, CA 94112 • 415-587-3416

Originally from Odessa in the Ukraine, Boris Levitt opened his small workroom in 1992 where he refinishes furniture and does custom upholstery work and caning. He also makes custom protective pads for dining tables. Attention to details has won Boris many loyal clients, including several San Francisco hotels and retail stores. Business hours are Monday through Friday 9 to 4 and Saturday 11 to 2.

ROSSI ANTIQUES

71 Williams Street • San Francisco, CA 94124
415-671-1144 • www.lxrossi.com

Born in Argentina and raised in Italy, Luis Rossi studied art history in Rome, followed by an apprenticeship at the Vatican Museum. Settling in San Francisco in 1980, he worked for a well-known antiques dealer for several years before opening his own atelier. Today, Luis and his small army of highly skilled artisans can restore or recreate a vast range of paint and lacquer finishes, as well as gilding, staining, waxing, carving, marquetry and metal in-lay, leather retooling, and distressed re-silvering for antique mirrors. They also work in exotic materials like ivory, coral and minerals. Luis has even developed a technique for disguising a plasma television screen without hiding it in a cabinet! Additionally, he designed a spectacular line of furniture sold in designer showrooms across the country. Monday through Friday 9 to 3:45.

WARREN'S ANTIQUES

375 Ninth Street • San Francisco, CA 94103 • 415-703-0303

In addition to carrying Asian antiques, Warren's principle business is furniture restoration and conversions. For example, if you'd like to convert an antique sideboard into a fabulous commode for your bathroom sink, Warren's can do the job, and do it beautifully. Open Monday through Friday 8 to 5 and Saturday 9 to 4.

QUALITY TOUCH
(See Furniture, In-Home Refinishing, Restoration & Repair)

FURNITURE, WICKER & CANE REPAIR

AH SAM
1290 Union Street • San Francisco, CA 94109 • 415-928-6830

Born and raised in San Francisco, Hazel Gong began learning the craft of caning when she was eight years old from her father who had established his business in 1937. Hazel continues his tradition of excellence today and works with both hand-woven and pre-woven caned pieces. Since caning is an organic material, each piece of caned furniture is different and each requires a different approach. I loved it when Hazel said, "I'm always meeting the most interesting chairs." By appointment.

JAFE CUSTOM FINISHING
(See Furniture Refinishing, Restoration & Repair)

LAZO'S CANING REPAIR
484 E. 14th Street • San Leandro, CA 94577
510-638-7415 • www.LazosCaningRepair.com

Born and raised in Nicaragua, Roberto Lazo was taken by the military at a young age and forced to fight in the 1980s. After he was wounded, making wicker furniture was part of his rehabilitation. In 1989 he came to the United States, and in 2000 he was able to start his own business. Roberto repairs paper rush, rattan, Danish cord and wicker furniture, as well as replacing cane seats using both hand and machine caning. In his spare time, he fabricates custom wicker and Seagrass furniture to sell in his workshop. He offers pick-up and delivery service for three or more pieces of furniture. Open Monday through Friday 9 to 5 and Saturday 9 to 2.

MARIN FURNITURE CLINIC

68 Woodland Avenue • San Rafael, CA 94901

415-459-1067

Owners James and Liddy Ingram have been in business since 1982. Known for re-finishing, repairing and restoring antique furniture, a large percentage of their business is repairing and replacing cane and rush seating, both by hand and machine. Brewer chairs have become a specialty, and because the client is able to unscrew the seats and chair backs, they can be replaced, repaired and returned relatively quickly. (They receive over 100 Brewer chair seats each month from all over the U.S.) James is also a furniture appraiser affiliated with the New England Society of Appraisers. Business hours are 9 to 5 Monday through Friday and Saturday 10 to 12:30.

NEW DIMENSIONS

(See Furniture, Outdoor Furniture Restoration)

RENAISSANCE FURNITURE RESTORATION

(See Furniture Refinishing, Restoration & Repair)

THE CANING SHOP

926 Gilman Street • Berkeley, CA 94702

510-527-5010 • www.caning.com

Jim Widess started his business in 1969 to repair damaged cane furniture. He and his staff now do restoration, painting, toning, staining and finishing of old wicker as well as repairing splint woven seats, Danish Cord, and rushing. In the fall of each year they offer classes on basketry, caning and gourd-crafting. Jim published *The Caner's Handbook* a few years ago and a second volume is due out in 2006. Hours are Tuesday through Friday 10 to 6 and Saturday 10 to 2.

G

GILDING

ISMAY, GRAVES & HOLLAND
(See Paint Finishes, Murals & Decorative Artwork)

KATIE MCCABE
(See Furniture Refinishing, Restoration & Repair)

ROSSI ANTIQUES
(See Furniture Refinishing, Restoration & Repair)

SAMANTHA RENKO
(See Paint Finishes, Murals & Decorative Artwork)

GLASS & MIRRORS

PAIGE GLASS
1531 Mission Street • San Francisco, CA 94103
415-621-5266

This venerable establishment was founded by Paul Paige in 1907 and has been in continuous operation by family members ever since. The current generation includes grandson Ken Paige and his son Matt. You will find not only all your glass and mirror needs met by their comprehensive services, you will also find a large art gallery on the premises, as well as an inventory of one-of-a-kind mirrors and objet d'art for sale. In addition, Paige Glass offers quality framing and other art services for clients in the know. Open Monday through Friday 8 to 5.

THEISEN GLASS

301 Potrero Avenue • San Francisco, CA 94103
415-861-6942 • www.theisenglass.com

Family-run Theisen Glass has served San Franciscans for over fifty years, thirty-five of them at this location. Whether for new construction or remodeling, Theisen Glass can provide the glass and installation, with a specialty in custom replacement work. Open Monday through Friday 8 to 4:30.

GLASS & PORCELAIN RESTORATION

DAVID SCHOENBROD

91 Rockridge Avenue • Daly City, CA 94105 • 650-992-8203

With a fascinating background in naval architecture, pre-med, and fine art, David ultimately found his niche in decorative art restoration in 1956. Today, he prefers working with small objet d'art like ceramics, glass, ivory, and semi-precious stone and does not handle paper or furniture. With his daughter Suzanne working at his side, David has been giving each item under his care the same extraordinary level of attention to detail for over fifty years. Call for an appointment.

SELJUK

38 Gough Street • San Francisco, CA 94103 • 415-863-1997

Seljuk works on leather, porcelain, jade, glass, ivory, metal, Oriental lacquer and screens, small sculptures, and ceramic figurines. He also does gold leafing and diamond drilling. You will need to remind yourself to pick up your items, because so many loyal clients keep him too busy to call. However, he tries to complete every job within a week. In business since 1959, Seljuk's customers come from all over the United States. Taped to a countertop in the shop is one of his favorite possessions—a photocopy of a check signed by Ronald Reagan for a repair job from the 1970s. Business hours are Monday through Friday 9 to 5.

WALTER LOLIGER
(See Clock & Watch Repair)

VENERABLE CLASSICS
645 Fourth Street, Suite 208 • Santa Rosa, CA 95404
707-575-3626 • venerable@prodigy.net

Established in 1985, Venerable Classics has restored over 15,000 pieces using a combination of handcraftsmanship and state of the art technology. Owner Janet Connolly and her artisans special-ize in museum-quality restoration of glassware, porcelain, jade, ivory, marble and other fragile materials. Call or email regard-ing estimates, shipping and, most important, the necessary steps for salvaging your broken treasure. By appointment only Monday through Friday 10 to 5.

Z.A. RESTORATION CO.
Pier 33 Embarcadero • San Francisco, CA 94111 • 415-693-9141

While still living in the Ukraine, Jane Kustura did restoration work for museums. Now she and her husband Anatoliy work out of a small shop on Pier 33. (Drive almost to the end of the pier, past the seafood wholesalers, then watch for a small sign on the right side, above a screen door.) Jane does remarkable conservation and restoration on porcelains, enamels, bronzes, glass, wood, leather, paintings, icons, ivory, and stone as well as furniture and textiles. They can repair almost anything and, when needed, can even mold or sculpt replacement parts that would be otherwise impossible to restore. Open 11 to 5 Monday through Friday and Saturday 11 to 4.

GLASS BLOWING

R & D GLASS PRODUCTS
1808 Harmon Street • Berkeley, CA 94703 • 510-547-6464

Founded in 1976 on the site of Berkeley's earliest movie theater, which operated between 1909 and 1912, the artisans at R & D will hand-blow any glass component, including custom glass chimneys for hurricane lamps, glass shades, and towel bars. Owner Douglas Dobson and his staff can repair crystal or cut glass vases, glass domes, antique stemware, beakers, decanters—just about anything in glass. Monday through Friday 8:30 to 5:30.

NIKOLAS WEINSTEIN
1649 Valencia • San Francisco, CA 94110
415-643-5418 • www.nikolas.net

Nik's passion is for creating large-scale commissions (customers for his glass sculptures include Gumps and Barney's). He also handles a steady flow of contract work with private clients, auction houses, and antiques dealers. He can copy, reproduce, and/or replace an entire fixture or its parts. But because custom glass blowing can be quite costly, it's important to recognize that your piece is either an investment or has great sentimental value before proceeding with restoration work. Stop by his studio Monday through Friday 8 to 5.

GOLD PRINTING

MONARCH GOLD PRINTING
1072 Bryant Street • San Francisco, CA 94103
415-626-5789

Chuck Prosek began learning the gold printing trade from his dad when he was ten years old. Today, he runs the business which has been in operation since 1948. Using a foil stamping process, Monarch will print on a wide range of materials, including leather, vinyl, paper and fabric. Their most frequent requests are for luggage tags, presentation portfolios, award ribbons, picture frames and albums, and cigar cases. Open Monday through Friday 8 to 4:30.

HANDYMAN

ANDRE MORENO
415-587-0124 • 415-902-3974 (cell)

Over the years, Andre has done so many jobs for me around my home I've actually lost count. He has installed shelves, painted walls, hung chandeliers, rewired lamps, fixed leaking faucets, calked windows and tiles, replaced door hardware and repaired just about anything else you can think of. He doesn't waste a lot of time and is prompt and dependable. What more can you ask?

BRETT BRYANT
1366 20th Avenue • San Francisco, CA 94122
415-806-9608 • brettSF@earthlink.net

Brett can assist you with anything pertaining to lighting, from changing light bulbs to hanging or cleaning chandeliers. He can provide transport for a fragile or awkward fixture in need off-site repair, and he will deliver a newly purchased fixture that would otherwise be challenging to get home. Brett will travel anywhere in the Bay Area.

CHRIS WILLERS
415-596-3800

Chris is one of those very conscientious workers who doesn't over-commit himself and always builds in an extra cushion of time to handle unforeseen problems or jobs the client may have forgotten to account for. Thanks to this system, Chris is never late for an appointment. His reliability combined with a wide range of skills keeps Chris at the top of my list.

JOHN HANFORD

282 18th Street, #6 • San Francisco, CA 94121

415-668-1716 • jhanford@mindspring.com

John especially enjoys fine carpentry work, such as building custom cabinets, fireplace mantles, and bookcases. Hanging doors and paintings, securing objects for earthquake proofing, assembling furniture, and installing locks, decorative hardware, and shelving are only a few of the projects he will complete for you. By appointment.

HARDWARE, ANTIQUE REPLICATION

CIRECAST, INC.

1700 Yosemite Ave. • San Francisco, CA 94124 • 415-822-3030

Peter Morenstein has been designing and manufacturing fine hardware since 1965. Using the lost wax casting process, Peter and his staff produce fixtures in 19th century styles with detailing so superb it is hard to believe it is newly made. Each piece is meticulously cast and then polished by hand. Cirecast also restores antique brass, bronze, iron, steel, gold and silver. Their work is so authentic they were commissioned to restore and retrofit all the decorative hardware in San Francisco's City Hall, one of the most beautiful examples of Beaux Arts architecture in the country. Hours are 8 to 6 Monday through Friday, although I recommend calling first.

HARDWARE SUPPLIES

CENTER HARDWARE

999 Mariposa • San Francisco, CA 94107 • 415-861-1800

In business for over 100 years, this independently owned and operated store can fulfill all your hardware, plumbing and electrical needs. The knowledgeable and helpful staff is ready and willing to assist you. Open Monday through Friday 7 to 5 and Saturday 8 to 4.

E. M. HUNDLEY HARDWARE

617 Bryant • San Francisco, CA • 94107
415-777-5050 • www.hundleyhardware.com

Featuring merchandise for both residential and commercial jobs, if there's a hardware heaven—this is it. If they don't have it, they will order it for you. Open Monday through Friday 8:00 to 4:30 and Saturday 9:00 to 12:30.

JACKSON'S HARDWARE

435 DuBois • San Rafael, CA 94912
415-454-3740 • www.JacksonsHardware.com

Founded in 1964 by H.C. Jackson, the business was purchased in 1998 by its employees. In addition to a vast and varied inventory, service is their number one priority. With a welcoming attitude and extensive training in the products they sell, staff members (owner/employees) will accompany customers through their entire transaction, from locating items to the payment at the check out counter. There are suggestion boxes and evaluation forms and customers are encouraged to critique the store and staff. Imagine that at one of the huge chain stores! Open Monday through Friday 6 to 6 and Saturday 8 to 5.

HAULER

HAULING, ETC.
415-441-1054

Bill Jackson is the man to call when you need that old carpet taken up and removed, or you've got to empty out your garage before you put your house up for sale. He is available seven days a week for all general hauling. Call for an on-site estimate.

1-800-GOT-JUNK?
www.1800gotjunk.com

They'll remove any non-hazardous materials that two people can lift. But they won't take asbestos, chemicals, oils or oil drums, paints or solvents. They will take junky rusty patio furniture, broken appliances, grass clippings and yard refuse, or construction debris left over from your "full-service" contractor. Call for more information and pricing.

HOLIDAY DECORATING

EUGENE ANTHONY
394 Kansas Street • San Francisco, CA 94103
415-934-9119

Provide Eugene with a home and a holiday—Christmas, Easter, Halloween, birthdays, weddings and anniversaries—and he will handle every detail of the magical transformation. His strength is envisioning exactly what the client has in mind. Eugene will return after the event to pack everything for storage. By appointment.

RON MORGAN

510-444-8140

—and—

LOOT

5358 College Avenue • Oakland, CA 94618 • 510-652-3996

You can usually find Ron at the Flower Mart by 3 A.M. looking for the best and most beautiful of everything available, whether it's for a "floral catering" job, as he likes to describe his work, or for his gorgeous gift/antique shop Loot. Ron gives floral decorating classes out of his shop, travels the country speaking to garden clubs (over 150 in 2005), and has published a book, with another underway. Call him for an appointment.

HOME DINING

DINING IN

Traci Higgins • 415-595-2052 • www.dininginsf.com

This former food stylist and personal chef was being referred to so many new families she saw a real need for Dining In, an affordable personalized meal-delivery service. Traci will create a custom menu to meet your family's specific tastes, then deliver the meals to your home (or office) on a weekly basis. As this book goes to press, Dining In provides this wonderful service to San Francisco, Berkeley, Oakland, Marin County and most of the Peninsula. Call for more information!

HOUSE PLANTS

KELLEY & ASSOCIATES

Patrick Kelley

609 Bay View Drive • Aptos, CA 95003

831-685-8221 • patrickkelley@sbcglobal.net

For over twenty-five years, Kelley & Associates have been providing top quality indoor plants and plant care from Pebble Beach to San Francisco. They also offer an orchid (and other blooming tropical plant) rotation service.

LIVING GREEN PLANTSCAPE DESIGN

150-C 15th Street • San Francisco, CA 94103

415-864-2251 • livgrn@pacbell.net

Davis Dalbok and his talented staff design and install interior and exterior landscaping of any size, however, one of their specialties is working with limited spaces, such as courtyards and terraces, using water elements and lush plantings. They also sell indoor plants of all kinds as well as garden-related accessories, and they offer maintenance services and color rotation programs for your home or office. Open Monday through Friday 9 to 5 and Saturday 10 to 5.

BEAUTIFUL ORCHIDS

3319 Sacramento Street • San Francisco, CA 94118

415-567-2443 • 1-877-267-2443

www.beautifulorchids.com

Founded in 1999, Beautiful Orchids is a premier provider of potted and fresh cut orchids available to ship anywhere in the U.S. They guarantee the quality of each orchid shipped and will gladly accept orchids returned for replacement or refund if they do not meet your expectations. Their showroom is open Monday through Friday 10 to 6 and Saturday 11 to 6.

CALIFORNIA ORCHIDS

415-868-0203 • www.californiaorchids.com

Located in coastal Marin County, California Orchids devotes its 15,000 square feet to developing orchid collections for their clients. Tending to nearly 20,000 plants while they are out of flower, the orchids are delivered when their blooming cycle begins. When they have finished, the plants are collected and boarded until the next blooming cycle. California Orchids serves San Francisco, Tiburon, Belvedere, Mill Valley and Sausalito with pick-up and delivery as well as selected services to clients in other areas. Call for more information.

ORCHIDMANIA

717 Paris Street • San Francisco, CA 94112
415-841-1678 • www.orchids.org

The not-for-profit OrchidMania began as a "garage sale" with a few members displaying a few donated orchids on upturned cardboard boxes. Today, 10,000 plants are donated annually and sold by volunteers every Sunday from 12 to 2 in a 1,500-square-foot greenhouse, called the Orchid Temple. Next door is the recently refurbished reference library and donation reception center. All orchid donations are tax deductible and benefit AIDS charities.

HOUSE PLANTS, SILK & DRIED

SILKS

1265 Folsom Street • San Francisco, CA 94103
415-431-4300 • www.silkplantation.com

Artificial plants, trees and flowers are offered for sale and rent to the trade and to the public at "trade" prices. Skillfully made to fool the eye, many are difficult to tell from live specimens. (I am especially impressed with their mini-ivy topiaries.) Silks also creates custom flower arrangements and carries a wide variety of containers, baskets, and accessories. Open Monday through Saturday 8 to 5.

HOUSE STAFFING

AUNT ANN'S NANNY, HOUSEKEEPER & ESTATE AGENCY

2722 Gough Street • San Francisco, CA 94123
415-749-3650 • www.in-housestaffing.com

Aunt Ann's has been placing nannies, housekeepers, personal chefs, butlers, estate managers, personal assistants and executive assistants in some of the finest homes in the San Francisco Bay Area since 1958. There is no registration fee and no fees at all until you have hired an employee through them.

A NANNY CONNECTION, INC.

P.O. Box 1038 • Danville, CA 94526
925-743-0587 • www.nannyconnection.com

Robin LeGrand's agency provides full- or part-time, live-in or live-out placements. She prides herself on her ability to find the perfect nanny for each family's specific needs. The agency offers "practice days" which places a candidate in the home with the family on a trail basis, as Robin feels this is the best way to ensure the right fit. Robin is usually in the office from Monday through Friday.

TOWN & COUNTRY

1388 Sutter Street, Suite 904 • San Francisco, CA 94109
415-567-0956

For over twenty years, Town & Country have been placing nannies, chefs, housekeepers, personal assistants, and baby nurses in homes all over the Bay Area. They offer staffing solutions including full-time, part-time, permanent and temporary placements. More than 85 percent of their clients come from personal referrals and repeat business. There is a registration fee plus a referral fee should you select one of their candidates. The office is open Monday through Friday 8:30 to 5:30.

HOUSE STAGING

ARTHUR MCLAUGHLIN & ASSOCIATES

1457 Baker Street • San Francisco, CA 94115
415-673-6746 • www.arthurmclaughlin.com

Decorating a home in order to sell it has a completely different goal than decorating it for highly personalized everyday living. Arthur McLaughlin knows how to make rooms appealing to a diverse range of tastes using the existing furnishings or by implementing an extensive makeover. Sometimes adding (or removing) just a few accessories or pieces of art is all it takes. I have never personally worked with Arthur. However, according to several of the top real estate agents in San Francisco, he is considered to be the best in his field with twenty years experience behind him.

KEN FULK INTERIORS

4104 24th Street #221 • San Francisco, CA 94114 • 415-285-1164

Ken is a busy interior designer who also offers full-service house staging. With warehouses full of furniture and accessories at the ready, Ken can make over an entire home right down to the bath towels! I promise, working with this low-key yet extremely talented young man will make the entire experience absolutely painless for you. Trust me on this one!

I

INTERIOR DESIGNER BUYING SERVICE

BUY DESIGN

110 Henry Adams Street, Suite 354 • San Francisco, CA 94102
415-626-4944 • buydesign@sbcglobal.net

Many interior decorators rely on referrals for new clients, but if you are new to the Bay Area and don't yet have friends to ask for decorator referrals, where do you start? Instead of living in an empty house or apartment, call Betsy Jaques to help you find the perfect furnishings at the San Francisco Design Center. She will take you through the showrooms and assist with purchases for a substantial savings off of the retail price. Since Betsy's hours are irregular because she is often out shopping with clients, be sure to call first to make an appointment.

INVITATIONS & STATIONERY, CUSTOM

ELIZABETH HUBBELL STUDIO

510-524-9898
elizabethhubbellstudio.com

Elizabeth Hubbell designs and creates invitations, announce-ments, stationery, business and note cards, the old-fashioned way—literally—on her 100-year-old printing press. She presses custom mixed inks onto beautiful textured papers imported from all over the world. Her work is elegant, refined, and completely unique. Contact her between 9 and 5 Monday through Friday.

JUST FOR FUN

3982 24th Street • San Francisco, CA 94114
415-285-4068 • www.justforfun.invitations.com

This neighborhood card and gift store has a superb stationery department that offers a vast selection of cards and five printing machines for creating personalized stationery with "almost-hand-written" calligraphy at reasonable prices. Another department creates custom invitations with private individuals as well as event planners. The store dogs, Digory Kirke, Rabadash and Tommy, greet customers Monday through Friday 9 to 8, Saturday 9 to 7 and Sunday 10 to 6.

IRON & METAL WORK

AKW METALS

277 Carolina Street • San Francisco, CA 94103
415-554-0911 • akwmetal@sbcglobal.net

Alex Weinstein is the proud owner of this machine shop and small foundry. With the help of two full-time employees Alex has provided high-quality custom metal work since 1995. He works with most metals, including bronze, steel, iron, titanium, and brass. In addition to fabrication and casting, he can assist you in the design of your project with full CAD renderings.

BLANK AND CABLES

(See Furniture, Metal)

I OFF

(See Furniture, Metal)

MARK NICHOLS
21720 Highway 29, #B • Middletown, CA 95461 • 707-987-0300

When Mark Nichols visited California in 1989 for a family wedding, he fell in love with the rural hills above Calistoga and decided to move himself and his blacksmith business from Minnesota to Middletown. Mark had learned his trade by age eighteen after taking a ferrier (horse shoeing) class. More than three decades later he is making iron gates and stairway railings, custom fireplace screens and table bases, as well as iron sculpture that is exhibited and sold in galleries throughout the wine country. Open Monday through Friday 8:30 to 5:30.

RENAISSANCE FORGE
47 Juniper • San Francisco, CA 94103 • 415-864-6033

Make an appointment to visit Renaissance Forge to see this home/forge/winery and to meet its unforgettable owner, Garro. Angelo, who can fabricate just about anything out of iron or bronze. And he will custom design everything from curtain rods to the gates of your wine cellar. And if you are very, very lucky, this renaissance man might ask you to sit down and sample some of his homemade wine or taste some of his Sicilian home cooking. Call first.

STANDARD SHEET METAL
366 Brannan Street • San Francisco, CA 94107
415-392-6495

Founded in 1942 by Joseph Bruno for industrial fabrication, today Standard Sheet Metal is run by Bruno's son Jim, and much of their work has shifted to residential and commercial custom projects. They enjoy working with architects and designers, and particularly love the "oddball jobs" that individual customers bring in. They ingeniously fabricate almost anything made with stainless steel, copper, aluminum, bronze or iron. Jim's son Mike has been working in the business since he was seventeen. Together they plan to continue offering the great service, integrity and friendship in the tradition of Joe Bruno. Open Monday through Friday 8 to 3:30.

WORDS AND MUSIC

1670 Abram Court • San Leandro, CA 94577
510-352-7770 • www.wordsandmusicdesign.com

When Rob Schmidt decided to pair his unabashed romanticism with an entrepreneurial background, he came up with a new business using his imagination, a computer, a plasma torch, and sheet metal. Rob replicates a client's favorite lyrics, quotations, or words in flat sheet-metal cutouts, ready to be hung on the walls of home and office. The choice may be a line from a much-quoted poem or special song, or an inspirational quote from a famous person or literary source. Rob will craft these words into a unique decorative creation that's ready to hang. He is usually in his studio Monday through Friday, but it is best to call for an appointment.

KNIFE SHARPENING

COLUMBUS CUTLERY
358 Columbus Avenue • San Francisco, CA 94133
415-362-1342

Philip Antoniolli and his wife Jenny are only the second owners of this over forty-year-old business that sharpens just about anything: kitchen and pocket knives, wire nippers, hair shears, meat slicers and grinders, cuisinart blades, gardening equipment such as lawn mower blades, pruning shears, chisels, even electric razors. Hours are 9:30 to 5. Closed Wednesdays and Sundays.

HIDA TOOL
1333 San Pablo • Berkeley, CA 94702 • 510-524-3700

Selling exclusively Japanese knives and hand tools, Hida Tools also offers a sharpening service for knives, carpentry and gardening tools using stones mined in Japan that achieve an especially hard-wearing and long-lasting edge. Imported Japanese sharpening stones are also available for purchase. Monday through Friday 9 to 5.

JIVANO'S CUTLERY SERVICE
3674 18th Street • San Francisco, CA 94110
415-552-7997 • www.jivano.com

Isn't it great to find a business that lists its prices right up front? At the front door of this tiny shop is the price list for all sharpening services. There is also a slot in the door where you can drop small items. Just leave your name and phone number and you'll get a call when they're ready for pick-up. It's a good idea to call before dropping by because Jivano makes house calls when sharpening costs total $50 and up. He also sells an eclectic inventory of knives.

KELLY'S EDGE SHARPENING

690-A Redwood Highway • Mill Valley, CA 94941

415-606-3343

Len Kelly works in a tiny 8 x 10 foot shack next to Green Jeans plant nursery. Accompanied by his dog Roxy, Len has been sharpening knives, scissors, beautician shears, pet clippers and garden tools in this location since 1999. Wednesday through Saturday 10 to 5 and Sunday 10 to 3.

THE CRITICAL EDGE

Bob Kattenburg • 925-937-3343

Bob Kattenburg drives his mobile sharpening shop all over the Bay Area throughout the week. Find him at the Ferry Plaza Farmers' Market in San Francisco on Saturdays from 8 to 2, the Walnut Creek Farmers' Market (in the Library parking lot) on the first and third Sundays from 9 to 1 and the El Cerrito Plaza Farmers' Market in El Cerrito Plaza (Southeast corner) on the second Tuesday of the month from 9 to 1 Twice a month he sets up at Andronicos Market in Danville, but the days change so call for an update. In addition to knives, Bob works on scissors, food processor blades and most hand-operated garden tools.

LAMPSHADES

DIBELLA LUCE
3664 Black Feather Drive • Richmond, CA 94803
510-758-4227 • www.dibellaluce.com

Ginger Takahashi has been creating unique lampshades since 2001. Inspired by a love of heirloom lighting and a passion for antique textiles, she creates custom shades, restores period bases and adds hand-beaded fringes for whimsical, rather over-the-top period-looking light fixtures. Custom designs to order are also welcome.

FORREST JONES
3274 Sacramento Street • San Francisco, CA 94115
415-567-2483

Frenchman Phillippe Henry de Tessan stocks 700-800 lampshades in silk, parchment, paper and linen in myriad sizes and shapes, along with a large selection of reasonably priced finials. He will also convert almost any object into a table lamp base, then find just the right shade and finial for it. In addition to doing minor lamp repairs, he also stocks ready-made lamp bases, as well as home accessories with a distinct European flair. Open Monday through Saturday 10 to 6 and Sunday 11 to 5.

LAMP GALLERY
628 Santa Cruz Avenue • Menlo Park, CA 94025
650-325-6585

The Lamp Gallery carries an extensive selection of lamps, shades and lighting accessories to complement any décor. They also fabricate custom lamps and will design a shade for you. Take a picture of what you would like and they will make it. Dee Skaar is their designer and a partner in the business. Open Tuesday through Friday 10 to 6 and Saturday 10 to 5.

LAMP SHADE HOUSE

120 Second Avenue • San Mateo, CA 94401 • 650-348-1158

When Alan Edwards retired, he sold his lampshade manufacturing company in southern California and moved to the Bay Area. His wife wanted him to keep busy so the Lamp Shade House was born in 1993, first in Burlingame and now in San Mateo. In addition to lamp repair and re-wiring, Alan will create the perfect custom shade in virtually any material. He also carries a selection of ready-made shades. Business hours are Tuesday through Friday 10:30 to 6 and Saturday 10:30 to 3.

SUE JOHNSON CUSTOM LAMPS & SHADES

1745 Solano Avenue • Berkeley, CA 94707
510-527-2623 • www.suejohnsonlamps.com

Sue is a lamp and lampshade designer who has been operating out of her small shop in Berkeley since 1975. Sue or one of her talented staff can make a lamp out of anything and design the perfect shade to accompany it. They work primarily in mica and parchment paper shades and can tint the paper any color, often sponging the tint onto the parchment for an unusual and richly textured look. Open Monday through Saturday 12 to 6 and Sunday noon to 5.

THUNDERDOG DESIGN

Eric Flaniken • 415-665-8220
www.thunderdogdesigns.com

Eric makes custom lampshades for any size or style lamp for interior decorators, antiques dealers, and individual clients. He works by appointment and will come to your home with fabric samples and sample wire frames. From a photo or a sketch he can create any shade and will gladly use your fabric if you prefer. Eric also collects vintage Japanese kimonos and obis from which he fabricates gorgeous lampshades.

LANDSCAPING SERVICES

GARDENER BRAD

584 Castro Street #248 • San Francisco, CA 94114
415-377-8173 • brad@gardnerbrad.com

Brad Frazier is extremely dependable for all landscaping and gardening challenges, including irrigation, maintenance, plant installation, pest control and nearly anything else garden-related. And when it's time to sell your house, he will enhance your outdoor property for the all-important "curb appeal."

LEATHER ARTISAN

APRIL IN PARIS

55 Clement Street • San Francisco, CA 94118
415-750-9910

Beatrice Amblard has more than twenty-three years experience in this unique field, and worked for many years with the Parisian House of Hermes. To date she is the only former Hermes designer to open her own shop in the United States. Beatrice does custom work only. Her design commissions include furniture, purses and other small leather goods, even automobile interiors! Tuesday through Saturday 11 to 5.

LEATHER CLEANING, REPAIR & ALTERATION

ANTHONY'S SHOE SERVICE
(See Shoe Repair & Dyeing)

LEATHER CARE CLEANERS
2345 Mission Street • San Francisco, CA 94110 • 415-647-2345

In business since 1975, Jack Kim is a leather specialist who can spot and clean anything in leather or suede from furniture to bedroom slippers and virtually anything in between. Many local dry cleaners out-source their leather work to Jack, who also does alterations and the custom dyeing. Open weekdays from 7:30 to 5:30 and Saturday 9 to 5.

WENDELS LEATHER SHOP
1623 Polk Street • San Francisco, CA 94109 • 415-474-4104

This specialty leather clothing store also offers leather cleaning, repairs, dyeing, and alteration services. Open Tuesday through Friday 11 to 5.

LEATHER RE-TOOLING

ROSSI ANTIQUES
(See Furniture Refinishing, Restoration & Repair)

LIGHTING

ALEX BARCLAY
1529 W. Cortez • Chicago, IL 60622 • 1-800-295-0559
www.bloominglites.com • question@bloominglites.com

Bloominglites specializes in locating replacement parts for chandeliers and lighting fixtures. Call or email Alex with your requirements and she will customize your order. She also makes whimsical glass and crystal lampshades in any size or color, as well as fun floral ceiling fixtures that make decorative replacements for conventional ceiling fixtures. Alex's daughter, Jessica Bodner, is also listed in this book (see Lighting Repair, Restoration & Wiring) and they often work together on special projects. When you call, remember the two-hour time difference between the Bay Area and Chicago!

CITY LIGHTS
1585 Folsom Street (at 12th St.) • San Francisco, CA 94103
415-863-2020

City Lights features the Bay Area's largest selection of decorative and architectural lighting fixtures, and also stocks a huge assortment of bulbs and other lighting accessories. Monday though Friday 8 to 5:30 and Saturday 9 to 5.

LIGHTING DESIGN & CONSULTATION

HIRAM BANKS
461 2nd Street, #659 • San Francisco, CA 94107
415-618-0855 • hiram@hebanks.com
www.hebanks.com

In business in San Francisco since 1989, Hiram approaches each commission with the goal of a seamless integration of structure and illumination so that the space or room or object is lit flawlessly—and invisibly. He works his magic in both residential and commercial spheres, including private homes, yachts, and jets, as well as hotels, restaurants and landscaping—virtually any venue that needs to be lit! The office is open 8:30 to 5:30 Monday through Friday.

ROBERT TRUAX
418 Petaluma Avenue • Sebastopol, CA 95472
707-829-8188 • bob@rtld.net

Bob Truax is considered to be one of the best lighting designers in the industry, not only in the Bay Area but throughout the world. His attention to detail, product and technical knowledge, and sheer creativity is legendary. Bob, and his talented team, do both residential and commercial work and are available for consultation by appointment.

LIGHTING REPAIR, RESTORATION & WIRING

BODNER CHANDELIERS
1660 Jerrold Avenue • San Francisco, CA 94124
415-641-1139 • bchandeliers@aol.com

Jessica Bodner draws rave reviews from decorators, whether they've used her for lighting restoration projects or commissioned her to design custom light fixtures. After twelve years in the business, Jessica is now able to incorporate two of her heart-felt passions, lighting and sculpture. Her workroom is open Monday through Thursday 9 to 3.

FORREST JONES, INC.
(See Lampshades)

KELVIN'S LIGHT SOURCE

1583 43rd Avenue • San Francisco, CA 94122
415-664-4892 • kelvinslightsource@yahoo.com

Kevin Ugar has been repairing antique chandeliers and lamps since 1985 and considers himself a serious craftsman. He will tackle any kind of lamp repair, rewiring or restoration. He also takes on custom lamp fabrication and designs to UL standards. By appointment.

LAMP GALLERY

(See Lampshades)

LAMP SHADE HOUSE

(See Lampshades)

LITE HOUSE HOME LIGHTING

4334 Geary Blvd. • San Francisco, CA 94118 • 415-221-4334

In business since 1960, John Clarke and his technicians repair antique light fixtures, expertly restoring them to original condition, including the original finish. They prefer to fashion parts from other fixtures rather than use new replacement parts. And although John claims not to be in the parts business, he does have a large collection of old sockets, globes, switches, and other parts that he sells on request. The Lite House also stocks restored antique lamps, chandeliers, and sconces, and a small inventory of new fixtures. Monday through Saturday 9:30 to 5.

SUE JOHNSON CUSTOM LAMPS & SHADES

(See Lampshades)

VICTOR'S LIGHTING

2166 Palou Avenue • San Francisco, CA 94124

415-285-1280 • info@victors-lighting.net

In business since 1947, Victor's carries table lamp bases and chandeliers as well as hard-to-find specialty parts (gas pipe fittings, canopies, chains, etc.) and provides custom design and fabrication services. Owners Michael Donnelly and Jennifer Lum are working very hard to maintain the long-time relationships the original Victor had with his clients. Open 9 to 4 Monday through Saturday.

WALNUT CREEK LAMP REPAIR

1800 Tice Valley Blvd. • Walnut Creek, CA 94595 • 925-933-5518

Established in 1989 by Tree Smith (that's really her name) this is the "candy store" for the home electrician. Tree stocks electrical and lighting hardware as well as replacement parts like switches, sockets, plugs, wiring, chain, harps, and crystals and decorative finials. She maintains a service department that repairs new and antique light fixtures. There is a nice selection of shades with sizes to order. Hours are varied: Closed Sunday and Monday, Tuesday noon to 5, Wednesday 10 to 6, Thursday and Friday 10 to 5.

YURY'S LIGHTS & BEYOND

1849 Divisadero St. • San Francisco, CA 94115 • 415-345-8660

Originally from Russia, Yuri opened his business in 2003. He gives very personalized service including highly skilled lamp and chandelier repair, restoration, and wiring. He also sells bulbs, glass shades, fabric shades, crystals and prisms. Hours are 9 to 6 Monday through Saturday.

LOCKSMITH

WARMAN SECURITY

1720 Sacramento Street • San Francisco, CA 94108
415-775-8513 • www.warmansecurity.com

Founded by Robert Warman in 1920, the business was purchased in 1942 by Homer Badertscher, passed on to his son John, and today is operated by his son Peter. In addition to lock installation and repair, Warman's sells cameras, burglar alarms, and security systems for residential and commercial clients. Monday through Friday 8:30 to 5 and Saturday 9 to 3. Emergency service is available at any time.

MIKE'S LOCKSMITH SERVICES

824 Cayuga Avenue • San Francisco, CA 94112 • 415-333 2233

Mike has been providing 24-hour, 7-days-a-week mobile emergency service for clients throughout the Bay Area since 1985. Whether you've been locked out of your house, need an extra set of keys or an assessment and estimate for a home or business security system, you will find Mike both knowledgeable and reliable.

LUGGAGE REPAIR

MAIN LUGGAGE SERVICE & REPAIR
1425 Bush Street • San Francisco, CA 94109 • 415-673-2286

Main Luggage has been providing an independent service to the luggage industry for over twenty years. They accept all airline claims and will service all brands and models of luggage, also handbags and briefcases. They will tackle virtually any kind of repair, including repairs to finicky key and combination locks. In an emergency, they will make every effort to provide rush service while you wait. Open Monday through Friday 9 to 5.

TONY'S SHOE REPAIR & LUGGAGE
(See Shoe Repair & Dyeing)

M

MATTRESS, CUSTOM

DREAMS
(See Pillow & Cushion Fabrication)

MCROSKEY AIRFLEX MATTRESS COMPANY
1687 Market Street • San Francisco, CA 94103
415-861-2616

In business in San Francisco since 1899, McCroskey's has a stellar reputation in the custom mattress business. In addition to superior custom mattresses, they sell trundle beds, sofa beds, pillows, comforters, bed linens, and crib mattresses. They have even created pet beds with removable slip covers. Open seven days a week.

MONOGRAMMING & EMBROIDERY

NG'S EMBROIDERY & SEWING DESIGNS
870 Market Street, #805 • San Francisco, CA 94102
415-986-3678

Sindy and Lai are sisters-in-law who went into business together in 1991. Located in the historic 1904 Flood Building, they embroider monograms for table, bath and bed linens, as well as clothing. They can design a monogram for you, or copy one from a drawing or photograph. They will work with most fabrics, including suede. On one occasion I noticed a project in progress in their workroom: it was a wedding gift commissioned by a frequent customer, a lovely pillow with the bride and groom's individual monograms entwined into one—and it was exquisite! Open Monday through Friday 10 to 5.

MOVE COORDINATION & ORGANIZING

TRANSITIONS
95 Fortuna Avenue • San Francisco, CA 94115
415- 675-0467

Paula Spooner offers three types of residential services: 1. She will plan your move, get you organized and ready for the move, then help you set up your new residence. 2. She will ready your home to be listed and sold, working closely with house stagers and real estate agents, so that it is shown to its maximum advantage. 3. She will reorganize your household before a major renovation, make recommendations for what you'll no longer need after the remodel, and help you pack up and store what you plan to keep. Paula has made the science of surviving a transition into an art. By appointment.

WINDDANCE
(See Organizing, Home & Business)

NEEDLEPOINT FINISHING

MARLENE CUSTOM PILLOWS, ETC.

1455 Bush Street, 2nd Floor • San Francisco, CA 94109
415-346-8112 • www.marlenecustompillows.com

Marlene Hobeck immigrated to the U.S. from Austria in 1967 and began finishing needlepoint pillows for Elaine Magnin Needlepoint in 1971. She opened her own studio in 1991. She still makes her own cords, fringes, tassels and ribbons and continues to custom dye threads in a mind-boggling array of colors. Marlene stocks a wide range of designer fabrics from which she makes custom pillows and recently introduced a unique gift wrapping idea: designer fabric bags in different sizes which, when tied with a silk cord and gift tag, presents a gift-within-a-gift that's both innovative and good for the environment, because the bag is reusable. Marlene's clients have been scooping them up! Monday through Friday 8:30 to 4:45.

O

ORGANIZING, HOME & BUSINESS

CALIFORNIA CLOSETS
2040 Union Street • San Francisco, CA 94123
415-921-2040 • www.calclosets.com

The aim of these experts is to help their clients go back into the closet! Whether it's a spacious walk-in or a cramped pantry, they offer practical solutions for maximizing existing space and reorganizing for efficient storage. A wide selection of surface finishes, colors, and architectural details to coordinate with your existing interiors are available. Initial consultations are free.

SAHINA - PERSONAL ORGANIZER
415-750-1241 • sahinasf@aol.com

Using the ancient concepts of feng shui, Sahina helps clients tackle the very modern problem of having too much stuff! For Sahina, clutter in the home represents blocked life energy in the homeowner. This can result in feeling overwhelmed or even paralyzed, particularly in the aftermath of a trauma such as divorce or death, or even a difficult move. Clients learn to use space more efficiently and let go of things that are no longer needed. By appointment.

TRANSITIONS
(See Move Coordination & Organizing)

WINDDANCE

Breeze Carlile
21 Macondray Lane • San Francisco, CA 94133
415-309-1860 • Breeze@WindDanceCo.com

Breeze has relocated and de-cluttered over 193,000 square feet of families! So if you are being relocated, she will manage the move at both origin and destination. She will also de-clutter your home, pack for the move, and manage the sale of unwanted items through consignment or auction. And if you just need to get your home or office organized, she will do that, too. Breeze is a member of the National Association of Professional Organizers.

ORIENTAL RUG REPAIR & CLEANING

J.M. COLLECTIONS

(See Textile Repair & Cleaning)

SIMONIAN ORIENTAL RUG CLEANERS

939 N. Amphlett Blvd. • San Mateo, CA 94401
650-343-0929 • joe@simonianrugs.com

Founded in 1956 by Mr. Simonian, the business was purchased and expanded by current owners Joseph and Araxi Bezkjian in 1978. In addition to repair, appraisal, and cleaning, they also buy and sell oriental rugs and tapestries. After going through a "dusting" machine, rugs are hand-washed, hand-rinsed, then put through a huge "wringer." Clean carpets are dried with air blowers and, weather permitting, placed outdoors in the sun. Pick up and delivery of large rugs is available. Open Monday through Friday 8 to 5 and Saturday 10 to 3.

SOHOYAN ORIENTAL RUG REPAIR
3100 Center Court Drive • Modesto, CA 95355
1-877-515-9125 • 208-551-6509

Sona learned the art of textile repair as a very young girl in her native Syria. In 1985 she moved to the Bay Area and began working for Soroya Rugs, a prestigious San Francisco oriental rug gallery. After a move to Modesto, she maintained her envied status as a master weaver, and continues to cater to Bay Area rug dealers, interior decorators, and their clients. In her modest warehouse she hand-washes carpets and tapestries, using no chemicals or drying heat, and skillfully repairs and conserves antique carpets and cushions. Sona drives to the Bay Area on Fridays for estimates, pick-ups and deliveries.

TALISMAN
(See Textile Repair & Cleaning)

ORNAMENTAL BUILDING MATERIALS

SAN FRANCISCO VICTORIANA, INC.
2070 Newcomb Avenue • San Francisco, CA 94124
415-648-0313 • www.sfvictoriana.com

In business since 1972, San Francisco Victoriana specializes in architectural molding and castings, suitable for restoration, remodeling, or new construction. Don't let the name fool you because they carry more than 350 styles of wood moldings from a wide variety of periods, as well as a large selection of embossed wallpaper borders, from original stock dating between 1890 and 1915, authenticated by the Smithsonian Institute. Open Monday through Friday 7:30 to 4.

PACKING, CRATING & SHIPPING

ENCLOSURES

1150 Illinois • San Francisco, CA 94107
415-826-3640 • operations@enclosures-dis.com

When you need anything crated, moved and/or stored, call Joaquin to help you with the arrangements. Rates are hourly based on how many workmen and trucks are required for the job. Storage fees are based on a per-cubic-foot per-month rate. Crating and shipping charges (to just about anywhere) are unique to the needs and destination of each job.

BOX WORLD

7022 Village Parkway • Dublin, CA 94568
925-833-0738 • 1-888-527-7225

This East Bay location stocks a full range of packaging, packing and moving materials, as well as gift boxes and mailing envelopes in every size you can imagine. Box World is an authorized shipping outlet for UPS and Fed Ex. Open Monday through Friday 9 to 5:30 and Saturday 10 to 4.

GENERAL CRATING

1031 25th Street • San Francisco, CA 94107
415-826-3400 • 415-826-3402 (fax)

In operation since 1990, General Crating handles fragile and/or awkward items of any size to any destination in the country or in the world. Start with a call or fax to Connie with a description, size estimate, and approximate value for insurance. Connie will follow up with a written estimate. Pending your approval, Connie will take care of the rest. Pick up within San Francisco is free. Crating, packing and shipping is usually same-day or next-day. Monday through Friday 8 to 4.

THE PACKAGING STORE

1255 Howard Street • San Francisco, CA 94103

415-558-8100

A great resource with a huge inventory of supplies and materials, they also carry seasonal gift-wrapping, do custom packing for shipping, and are both UPS and Fed Ex authorized outlets. There is always a notary on staff. Monday through Friday 8:30 to 5:30 and Saturday 9 to 5.

PAINT FINISHES, MURALS & DECORATIVE ARTWORK

ANTOINETTE BARONESSE VON GRONE

76 Alexander Avenue • San Rafael, CA 94901

415-256-8100 • vongrone@pacbell.net

Antoinette really is a Baronesse from northern Germany as well as a talented muralist. After studying haute couture in Paris and painting silk scarves for Hermes, she moved to Morocco, then Mexico, then Greece, and then back to Germany. She subsequently discovered California and now claims it as her own. Today, her oil paintings, murals and ceramics reflect the influence of her nomadic background. Antoinette's work is bold and rich and vibrant. Her studio is in her home, so contact her Monday through Saturday from 9 to 7.

CARLO MARCHIORI

Ca'Toga Galleria D'Arte
1206 Cedar • Calistoga, CA 94515 • 707-942-3900

Where do I start? Being part of Carlo Marchiori's life is like a trip on the Mad Hatter's ride at Disneyland—you emerge feeling dizzy, yet wondrously energized and aware of feeling very privileged because you've been part of a fantasy that you simply can't describe to anyone who hasn't been there. Born and trained in Vicenza, Italy, Carlo came to California in 1975 and has been prolifically producing paintings and sculpture ever since. Famous for his whimsical trompe l'oeil murals, Carlo has an entourage of faithful devotees. His atelier is in his home, however, he also has a gallery in Calistoga where you can experience his work and, if you are very lucky, he will be there on the day you visit. Open from 11 to 6 Thursday through Monday, or by appointment.

ISMAY, GRAVES & HOLLAND

1777 Alemany Boulevard • San Francisco, CA 94112
415-334-5772 • www.studioigh.com

Eric Ismay, Warner Graves and Hugh Holland offer a fascinating variety of painted finishes, including Gustavian, Venetian, Chinoiserie, trompe l'oeil, grisaille, faux bois, pen work, milk paint, and a wide range of period painting and gilding styles and designs for authentic restoration work. Open Monday through Friday 9:30 to 3.

KATHERINE JACOBUS

46A Langton Street • San Francisco, CA 94103
415-241-9331

Katherine came to the "faux finish" world after earning her BFA in illustration at the famed Parsons School of Design in New York. An interest in interior design led her to decorative painting and, as they say, the rest is history. Since moving to San Francisco, she has gained the trust and respect of interior decorators as well as private clients. Katherine enjoys playing with finishes, creating tromp l'oeil paintings and murals, and loves and understands the world of antiques. By appointment.

MICHAEL DUTÉ FINE ART INTERIORS
632 Hayes Street • San Francisco, CA 94102
415-554-0124 • www.michaeldute.com

Michael Duté is one of the premier artists in the Bay Area whose passion for residential painted interiors is rooted in a strong European tradition. His own home is a resplendent display of his talents, with each room portraying a different historical theme, including a delightful Chinoiserie library with a pagoda-style bookcase and a richly textured Pompeiin bedroom. Michael works throughout California and beyond.

WOODMAN DESIGNS
632 Cole Street • San Francisco, CA 94117
415-225-5052 • www.woodmandesigns.net

San Francisco native Pilar Woodman opened her studio in 2001 and shortly thereafter was joined by her sister Andie. They produce marvelous specialty finishes, faux painting, gold leafing, stenciling, painted furniture restoration and services that include repair and restoration of original finishes in period homes. These talented young women work all over the Bay Area and have completed projects in Hawaii and Los Angeles.

RUBY NEWMAN
90 Purrington Road • Petaluma, CA 94952 • 707-765-6824

Since 1973, Ruby has enjoyed designing and producing murals and trompe l'oeil effects in classical, contemporary and even abstract styles. Her murals are produced on canvas at her studio and professionally installed on your site. She also creates faux finishes and specializes in exterior and interior color consulting. This talented artist has won numerous awards for her many residential and commercial commissions.

SAMANTHA RENKO

415-332-3293

Known primarily for her lovely floral murals, Samantha also enjoys creating decorative finishes on furniture as well as delicate hand-painting on porcelain. In addition to her hand-painted dinner plates, I particularly love her exquisitely decorated small porcelain boxes. Samantha recently took up portraiture and has a new interest in the restoration of antique painted screens. By appointment.

THE HELIOTROPE STUDIO

920 Willow Street • Alameda, CA 94501 • 510-522-6590

After a fifteen-year career as an architect, in 1990 Deirdre McCartney began creating trompe l'oeil, faux finishes, floor painting, and painted furniture in 1990. I think she enjoys painting murals more than anything else and her use of perspective is remarkable. A happy client once recommended, "Call Deirdre—she'll make a scene in your home." I love it!

PAINTING CONTRACTORS

OLD WORLD FINISHES

24 Skylark Drive #24 • Larkspur, CA 94939
415-927-2718 • rpsieg@owfd.com

Richard Sieg has been painting Bay Area homes since 1987. However, Richard is more than just a housepainter. After carefully stripping and reconditioning the underlying wood, he thoughtfully researches colors and products before picking up a paintbrush. Richard specializes in oil-based finishes and also does specialty painting and finishing on furniture.

PICTURE PERFECT
P.O. Box 1011 • Tiburon, CA 94920
415-207-1775 • www.pictureperfectpainting.com

After earning a Master's degree in English from Harvard, Richard Taylor arrived in San Francisco and couldn't find a teaching job. A friend found him work with a painting contractor, which Richard discovered he really enjoyed. When a teaching position finally became available, he stopped painting for several years, but returned to it for financial reasons. (That's right—I'm sad to say, there's more money in house painting than teaching!) Richard's company offers exceptional quality work at reasonable prices. Richard also consults on interior and exterior color design.

RAMIRO LOMELI
P.O. Box 305 • Novato, CA 94948 • 707-552-1220

Ramiro and his small crew have been working all over the Bay Area since 1997. He does interior and exterior painting, wood preservation for decks, wallpaper removal, power washing, and drywall repair. Call for a free estimate.

PARTY, EVENT PLANNERS

ATMOSPHERES BY JOSEPH CUNNINGHAM
3876 Sacramento Street • San Francisco, CA 94118
415-668-2112 • www.atmospheresjc.com

Joey Cunningham does innovative event design for weddings, holiday celebrations, and gala events, private and corporate, throughout the Bay Area. He has organized events in Mexico, Los Angeles and even Europe for his devoted wine country clients. In the business for almost twenty years, he takes care of the flowers, table linens, works with lighting designer, caterer, etc. I've seen him work on a tight budget (my friend's intimate wedding) or a generous budget (the Napa Valley Wine Auction and a Dreamworks Studio gala).

ROBERT W, FOUNTAIN

300 De Haro Street, Suite 342 • San Francisco, CA 94103
415-934-6767 • www.robertfountain.com

Robert Fountain refers to his work as "event architecture" but for purposes of this book, I decided to use the name by which people will most easily recognize his services—party planner. For such a young man, Robert has a sophisticated sense of style and unshakable confidence. He offers event planning for any size or budget and he will handle even the smallest details. His first love is floral design so you can be sure the flowers will be spectacular! Call for a consultation.

SUSAN MOSELEY

(See Catering)

PARTY MUSIC

BAGUETTE QUARTETTE

P.O. Box 7685 • Berkeley, CA 94707
510-528-3723 • www.baguettequartette.org

This Bay Area band plays music reminiscent of Parisian cafes and dancehalls in the 1920s, 30s, and 40s. Their musical arrangements include valses, musettes, tangos, pasos dobles, fox trots, etc., and manages to be distinctive, heart wrenching, jazzy, and melancholy—all at the same time. You will love it!

JASON MYERS

P.O. Box 2024 • El Cerrito, CA 94530-2024 • 510-524-4423

Jason is one of my favorite entertainers in the Bay Area. Versatile, friendly, and accommodating, he is a fabulous pianist with a great group of musicians to back him up. He can provide solo piano or up to a quintet with vocalist. Jazz standards from the 1930s and 40s are his specialty. I wouldn't think of having a party without Jason!

RICH MARTINI ORCHESTRA
650-348-7972

The Rich Martini Orchestra pride themselves on being the perfect party band. Performing for over ten years all over the Bay Area, they have collected a vast repertoire of music that'll get a crowd on its feet and turns a party into an event. They can be booked through Associated Entertainment Consultants (see the number listed above).

ROYAL JAZZ SOCIETY ORCHESTRA
P.O. Box 750663 • Petaluma, CA 94975 • 1-800-371-7756

Don Neely and the ten-piece Royal Society Jazz Orchestra are renowned for capturing the essence of 1920s and 30s swing and jazz. Their approach is fresh and exciting. For smaller events they can downsize to a superb sextet and for intimate gatherings they can provide a quartet or trio.

SONYA JASON
P.O. Box 370633 • Montara, CA 94037
650-563-9155 • saxtigress@aol.com
Sonya@sonyajason.com

This gifted sax player receives rave reviews wherever she performs and will happily connect with other musicians to form a variety of ensembles. For a cocktail party, she might offer a guitar, piano, sax jazz combo playing standards by Porter and Gershwin. For a garden party, she might suggest a soothing merger of sax, harp or flute performing a Baroque bouquet of Bach and Handel or a more classical repertoire of Mozart and Debussy. Her creativity and versatility are her hallmarks.

PARTY PHOTOGRAPHER

JOHN MARTIN

324 Valdez Avenue • Half Moon Bay, Ca. 94019
650-712-0752 • 925-980-8528 (cell) • jmarteen@pacbell.net

John will readily make himself available to photograph your next party or event. Your guests will like him because he is very personable and it is apparent that he loves what he is doing. John has a special talent for putting people at ease, they respond to his good nature, and the results are terrific party pictures. He will shoot both digital and 35mm photographs. I've used him many times!

PARTY RENTALS

CLASSIC PARTY RENTALS

1635 Rollins Road #A • Burlingame, CA 94010
650-366-7951 • www.classicpartyrental.com

Classic Party has a huge inventory and is considered to be one of the best service and equipment providers in the industry. Their maxim is "better-than-average quality with lower-than-average prices". Stock ranges from commercial refrigerators, freezers and stoves to chiavari chairs, linens, china, fine crystal, etc.

SF PARTY

939 Post Street • San Francisco, CA 94109
415-931-9393 • www.sfparty.com

SF Party provides everything that makes a party fun, from cotton candy, margaritas, and popcorn machines to balloons and games. Open Monday through Friday 8:30 to 6 and Saturday 10 to 4.

PIANO TUNERS

ALEX VAYN
415-731-6373 • www.alexpianotuning.com

With nearly thirty experience, Alex Vayn is the piano technician with the San Francisco Opera House and the Ballet Academy of San Francisco. This graduate of the Kiev School of Piano Tuning and Building in the former Soviet Union services, tunes, re-builds and repairs any size or any age piano.

LARRY NEWHOUSE
503 Ethel Avenue • Mill Valley, CA 94941 • 415-383-7690

Larry has been in the piano tuning and restoration business since 1974. He trained in Boston and later worked at the Steinway factory. He has maintained pianos at the San Francisco Conservatory since 1990. And if you're in the market for a piano, Larry can help you find the right instrument for you.

MARTIN SHEPARD
650-365-6681

Martin has been a piano tuner since the 1970s. Prior to that he worked for Steinway & Co. in New York. He is a member of the Piano Technicians Guild and is in demand by many institutions to care for their pianos, including the San Mateo Performing Arts, Memorial Hall at Stanford and Santa Clara University. By appointment.

THE PIANO CARE CO.
2011 Divisadero Street • San Francisco, CA 94115
415-567-1880

John Schaecher has been tuning pianos for over thirty years from the San Francisco Ballet and Symphony to the Plush Room on Sutter Street. He works in San Francisco only, making house calls Tuesday through Friday by appointment.

PILLOW & CUSHION FABRICATION

ANGELIQUE'S INTERIORS
(See Window, Curtain & Draperies)

DREAMS
921 Howard Street • San Francisco, CA 94103
415-543-1800

Dreams creates and/or stocks everything for the bed, including duvets, featherbeds, dust ruffles, pillow shams, bedspreads, even upholstered headboards. There is a mattress workroom on the upper floor where they manufacture standard or custom sizes. Because they do not recommend dry cleaning down products, they provide a down cleaning service. They also offer an unusual renovation service for down duvets, comforters, and pillows in need of plumping up with more down filling or requiring other repairs. Open Monday through Friday 10 to 6:30 and Saturday noon to 5.

MARLENE CUSTOM PILLOWS, ETC.
(See Needlepoint Finishing)

SHIRLEY ANDERSON
415-861-6920 • 415-810-9216 (cell)

Shirley designs and creates custom decorative pillows, bolsters, seat cushions, window seat pads, tablecloths, and bedding. Shirley has been working with local decorators for more than a decade and greatly enjoys working with private clients as well. You will be impressed by her reasonable prices and high-quality workmanship. By appointment.

PILLOW & CUSHION INSERTS

CUSHION WORKS
3320 18th Street • San Francisco, CA 94110
415-552-6220 • cushionworks@aol.com

Custom manufacturing is the backbone of this small business.
They carry standard sizes, but will custom cut or fill each piece
to fit. Not sure about the density you want? They have samples for
you to sit on, feel or try out. In addition to polyester, kapok and
down for cushions, they also stock upholstery supplies, including
welting, zippers, foam, thread, and batting to help do-it-yourself
upholsterers get started. Open 8 to 4:30 Monday through Friday.

DOWN ETC.
228 Townsend Street • San Francisco, CA 94107
415-348-0084 • sfdownetc@earthlink.net

This company provides luxurious bedding for many San Francisco,
Bay Area, and wine country hotels. Their downtown San Francisco
workroom stocks top-quality down pillows, comforters, and featherbeds in every size imaginable. Everything is 100 percent cotton,
double-stitched, and filled with prime white goose down. They will
manufacture custom sizes for large orders and ship anywhere.
Open 9 to 6 Monday through Friday, but this is a busy workroom,
so it's a good idea to make an appointment before stopping by.

PLASTER, ORNAMENTAL

LORNA KOLLMEYER
P.O. Box 1841 • San Francisco, CA 94188
415-822-6269 • info@lornakollmeyer.com

Lorna has been repairing, replacing, and recreating architectural
plaster elements since 1983 and cherishes her role in the preservation of the historical integrity of Bay Area buildings. Lorna can

replicate missing details from a Mediterranean-style mantel, or she can start from scratch and make a Victorian floral ceiling medallion. Basically, if it can be made in plaster, Lorna can make it!

PLASTER, VENETIAN

HANG IT UP TIM
(See Wall Upholstery)

OLEA PLASTERING
2139 Keith Street • San Francisco, CA 94124
415-822-7177

Tony Olea established his company in 1981. Over the decades he has perfected the exacting techniques required for Venetian plasterwork. His results are so dramatic and impressive that Tony is in constant demand to work his special brand of magic.

R

RECYCLING, APPLIANCES

CASEBER WASHERS & DRYERS
1908 Tenth Street • Berkeley, CA 94710
510-548-4419

Established in 1974, Caseber accepts used washers and dryers to refurbish and re-sell. As a member of the Citizens Opposing Polluting Environments (COPE) owner Jami Caseber is concerned with environmental issues and this is his way of contributing to his community. Because each appliance is reconditioned to virtually new, with warranties for labor and replacement parts, Jami says the only difference between refurbished and brand new is in the aesthetics. Tuesday through Saturday 9 to 5.

OUT OF THE CLOSET
1-800-558-8220 • www.aidshealth.org

Benefiting the AIDS Healthcare Foundation, Out of the Closet will pick up donated large appliances in clean and saleable condition. They have three locations in San Francisco—Church Street, Mission Street, and Polk Street—and one in Berkeley on University Avenue. All locations are open seven days a week.

RESTORE
(See Architectural Salvage)

RECYCLING, COMPUTERS

COMPUTER RECYCLING CENTER
1-888-887-3372 • www.crc.org

The Center accepts all models and brands of computers (monitors, keyboards, drives, laptops), telephones, cell phones, as well as miscellaneous electronic parts and equipment, in working or non-working order. Call or visit the website for drop-off locations. They will pick up large corporate donations of multiple machines. You can even mail your laptop and obtain reimbursement for the postage (see the website for instructions). Your donations are fully tax deductible, and refurbished equipment goes to teachers, schools, and non-profit community programs all over the Bay Area.

OAKLAND TECHNOLOGY EXCHANGE WEST
1680 14th Street • Oakland, CA 94607
510-893-4822 • www.otxwest.org

Donated computers and associated equipment are distributed to Bay Area schools and individual students. Donations are accepted Tuesday afternoons from 2:30 to 6, or by appointment, and are tax deductible. All donated equipment must be in working order.

RENEW COMPUTERS
1241 Anderson Drive, #J • San Rafael, CA 94901
415-457-8801 • www.renewcomputers.com

Renew Computers has been repairing and reselling donated computers since 1988. The proceeds go to various local charities. They also accept fax machines and cell phones. Computers older than a Mac G3 or a Windows 98 PC will have a recycling fee attached to it. Monday through Friday 9 to 5.

RECYCLING, KITCHEN APPURTENANCES

COOKIN'
339 Divisadero • San Francisco, CA 94117 • 415-861-1854

If it belongs in a kitchen and Judith Kaminsky doesn't have one in her small but cleverly organized 2,500 square-foot location, she can probably find it for you. Her astonishing inventory includes copper cookware, fondue pots (remember the 70s?), pyrex dishes in every shape and size, specialized bakeware, measuring and mixing bowl sets, hundreds of whisks, cookie guns, vintage salt and pepper shakers, and every imaginable kitchen gadget, to name a few. You will also find shelves full of cookbooks, many out of print. Judy has been collecting, recycling, and reselling kitchenware and associated items since 1981. Open Tuesday through Saturday 12 to 6:30 and Sunday 1 to 5.

RECYCLING, MATTRESSES

WALDEN HOUSE
520 Townsend Street • San Francisco, CA 94103
415-554-1100 • www.waldenhouse.org

Thanks to strict sanitation laws, it isn't easy to get rid of a mattress. However, Walden House, a drug and alcohol treatment center, gratefully accepts and distributes donated mattresses and bedding to needy Bay Area citizens. In fact, they accept donations of all kinds so keep them in mind the next time you clean out your home or garage.

ECUMENICAL HUNGER PROGRAM
2411 Pulgas Avenue • East Palo Alto, CA 94303 • 650-323-7781

This Peninsula organization operates a warehouse that distributes all kinds of home furnishings to low-income families at no cost—including mattresses.

RESOURCE SPECIALIST

GOFER UNLIMITED
2527 Gough Street • San Francisco, CA 94123
415-771-9899 • sfgofer@yahoo.com

Vicky Berol locates antique hardware, period lighting fixtures, and architectural details for decorators, contractors, architects, and private clients. Her specialty is matching existing hardware from as early as 1880 to the present day. There is no job too big or too small for her to tackle and fees are flexible.

ROOM MAKEOVER

DISTINCTIVE NEST
454 Las Gallinas Avenue • San Rafael, CA 94903
415-883-3017 • info@distinctivenest.com

Known as the "six-hour makeover ladies" the mother/daughter team of Susan Lahr and Sara Hunt Malone will come to your home and make over a room. An initial in-home consultation comes first to assess the room and your existing furnishings and accessories. Then, in just one day, they will create a "new" interior with things you already have. This dynamic duo charges by the hour and will work all over the Bay Area including Santa Rosa and Sacramento.

S

SHOE REPAIR & DYEING

ANTHONY'S SHOE SERVICE

30 Geary Street • San Francisco, CA 94108 • 415-781-1338

Established in 1920 and purchased by the Gentile family in 1966, brothers Gino and Mario offer friendly, high-quality service and will tackle any repair challenge. So don't throw out those favorite shoes you can't replace and thought were beyond repair. Open Monday through Friday 8 to 5:30 and Saturday 9 to 5.

FRANKS SHOE REPAIR

1619 Polk Street • San Francisco, CA 94109 • 415-775-1694

In business since 1934, Franks has had three locations, all on Polk Street. They do sole and heel repair, total shoe restoration, as well as polishing, cleaning, waterproofing and custom dyeing. They also repair and restore handbags and belts. Monday through Saturday 8:30 to 7.

TONY'S SHOE REPAIR AND LUGGAGE

38 Corte Madera Avenue • Mill Valley, CA 94941 • 415-388-5935

Tony's has been a shoe repair service since the mid-1950s and was purchased in 1970 by Misak Pirinjian. The high standard set by the original Tony continues today with quality renovation and restoration of shoes, luggage, handbags, and jackets. Open Monday through Friday 9 to 6 and Saturday 9 to 4.

SILVER MATCHING

MAXWELL SILVER MATCHING SERVICE
5690 Feather River Place • Paradise, CA 95969 • 530-872-7330

Tom Maxwell buys and sells estate silver and will fill out any active pattern. He also enjoys the challenge of hunting down obscure pieces or inactive patterns. In addition, he offers professional polishing services which can be a godsend if you've just inherited your grandmother's service for twenty-four that hasn't been touched since 1924!

SLIPCOVERS, CUSTOM

CHIOSSO BROS.
(See Upholstery)

JESENNIE'S UPHOLSTERY
(See Upholstery)

RAFAEL INTERIORS
(See Upholstery)

SANTA CRUZ SLIPCOVERS
3820 Enos Avenue • Oakland, CA 94619 • 415-819-1823

I'd heard good things about Santa Cruz Slipcovers but decided it was too far away to include in this book. When Jeanne Henzel relocated her business to Oakland, my quandary was resolved! After years as a theatrical costumer, Jeanne started a slipcover business in 2000. Today she also makes custom draperies, window seat pads, and pillows. Jeanne makes homes visits, where she does the actual cutting, then completes the job back in her workshop, returning in a week or so with the finished slipcover.

SUZANNE KING SLIPCOVERS
P.O. Box 582 • Mill Valley, CA 94942 • 415-388-2407

Suzanne has been making slipcovers since 1983 at her small studio in Mill Valley. She will give you the yardage requirements by phone, come to your home for the measuring and cutting, then completes the job at her studio. Suzanne uses heat-resistant zippers so your slipcovers are machine washable for easy maintenance.

SPEAKER REPAIR

A BROWN SOUN
23 Joseph Court • San Rafael, CA 94903
415-479-2124 • www.tonetubby.com

In business since 1974, keyboard player John Harrison couldn't find anyone to fix his blown speaker, so he repaired it himself. Today he runs a thriving business catering to musical artists like Neil Young, The Grateful Dead, and Metallica as well as corporate clients such as Lucasfilm and Dolby Studios. But you don't have to be famous to take your speakers to John. Open Monday through Friday 10 to 5:30. Saturdays 10 to 3:30 for drop-off and pick-up delivery only.

STAIR MAKER

JACK MEALY
757 Lincoln Ave. #24 • San Rafael, CA 94901 • 415-596-6646

The son of a man who "spoke fluent work bench," Jack Mealy taught himself to carve wood and make furniture by reading books about legendary cabinetmakers and their work. Today, Jack does some of the most inspired woodworking I have ever seen! Not only is he a skilled stair maker (carved balusters, handrails, newel posts, etc.) he also creates unusual window and door frames as well as furniture and wood sculpture. It's a good idea to call before you drop by.

T

TEXTILE REPAIR & CLEANING

J.M. COLLECTIONS
650-868-6045 • 831-595-5509 (cell)

Jack and Marie Sfeir are experts in the field of restoration and conservation of European tapestries, Aubusson and Oriental rugs, as well as high-quality textile cleaning. Maria also enjoys restoring antique embroidery and needlepoint. Business hours are flexible and they make house calls. Pick-up and delivery is offered all over the Bay Area and Monterey County.

TALISMAN
719 Swift Street #10 • Santa Cruz, CA 95060
831-425-7847

David Walker started the business in 1980 thanks to a keen interest in antique and ethnographic textiles. Today, Talisman is used by major museums all over the world for top-quality textile conservation, stabilization and display mounting. They also clean, restore, and re-line antique and modern tapestries, and they clean and repair handmade and machine-made rugs. Their reputation is so sterling they have never had to advertise. Every Wednesday, they pick up and deliver to San Francisco, the East Bay and Marin. On Thursday, they pick up and deliver to San Francisco and the Peninsula. Santa Cruz hours are Monday through Thursday 9 to 5 and Friday 9 to 3.

TILE PAINTING

TILE GALLERIA

4241 Norwalk Drive #Z302 • San Jose, CA 95129

650-814-0725 • www.tilegalleria.com

A graduate of the University of Padova, Italy, Sherry Saffarnia is a 21st century artist who started her career in 2005 creating exquisitely hand-painted tile murals inspired by 16th and 17th century European masterpieces. She also hand paints original contemporary designs on tile. Call for an appointment.

UPHOLSTERY

CHIOSSO BROS.
40 12th Street • San Francisco, CA 94103
415-431-5444 • jrchiosso@aol.com

Chiosso Bros. has been fabricating custom upholstered furniture since 1939. They will work from drawings or photographs and use the highest quality materials, like alder and other popular hardwoods, top brand coil springs, cottons, foams, and down. Locating this address can be tricky: Park on 12th and walk to Stevenson Street, which is more like an alley. You will enter Chiosso Bros. from Stevenson through the open garage doors. Their workroom is upstairs. Open Monday through Friday 8 to 4:30.

DREAMS
(See Pillow & Cushion Fabrication)

JESENNIE'S UPHOLSTERY
1319 Oat Crest Way • Antioch, CA 94531
1-800-820-0028 • jjuph98@aol.com

Mario Leon does the furniture upholstery while his wife, Mary, is the slipcover specialist. Send them a photo and dimensions and they will get back to you with yardage requirements. For upholstery work, they will pick up and deliver your furniture at no charge. For slipcovers, Mary will come to your home, make a template and return the finished slipcover to you in only a few days. They cover the East Bay, North Bay, the Peninsula, Contra Costa County, and San Francisco.

KAY CHESTERFIELD

6365 Coliseum Way • Oakland, CA 94621

510-533-5565 • info@reupholster.com

Since Jo Anne and John Jones purchased the business in 1990, they have maintained the tradition of quality workmanship and service started by the Kay family back in 1921. They enjoy the unusual distinction of a recommendation by a leading furniture manufacturer for their skill at handling challenging mid-20th century pieces (like Eames chairs). Send a photo with dimensions for a yardage estimate, or make an appointment for a house call. They will pick up and deliver for a modest fee. Open Monday through Friday 9 to 5 and Saturday 9 to noon.

KEVIN G.'S CUSTOM UPHOLSTERY

2648 3rd Street • San Francisco, CA 94107

415-643-4531 • kevingupholstery@aol.com

Kevin and his wife, Sezgi, have been in business since 1997 after Kevin served a sixteen-year apprenticeship under the watchful eye of a leading San Francisco upholsterer. He will fabricate furniture from a photo with dimensions or re-upholster your existing pieces for an entirely new look and feel. Open 8:30 to 5 Monday through Friday and Saturday by appointment.

KNOPS UPHOLSTERY SHOP

460 East 14th Street • San Leandro, CA 94577

510-635-2896

Originally established in 1958, Jose and Margarita Rodriguez bought the business in 1988. Jose trained at the well-known National Upholstery Company for twenty years. Today, thanks to his keen eye (Jose considers upholstery an art form), his work is considered to be among the best by many Bay Area decorators . Open Monday through Friday 7 to 4 and Saturday 7 to 10.

MATT O'REILLY

533 San Pablo Avenue • Albany, CA 94706 • 510-558-7403

Matt has been in the business of custom furniture upholstery since 1985. Take a drawing or photo to him and he will make it for you! Matt is meticulous about the quality of every piece of furniture that leaves his workroom, whether it's a wingback chair he built from scratch, a re-upholstered side chair, or even a slipcover. Monday through Saturday 7 to 3:30.

MATT STOICH

274 Magnolia • Larkspur, CA 94939 • 415-927-2362

Matt and wife Linda's workshop is the cute little yellow house next door to the Lark Creek Inn. In addition to re-upholstery, they fabricate new furniture, and make pillows and slipcovers. They are so particular about the quality of their work that, unlike many upholsterers, they insist each piece of furniture be brought to their shop, even for slipcovers! And when you bring in a photo for a new piece, Matt will make to-scale drawings on his computer before any work is begun. Their hours are 6 to 4 Monday through Friday.

OLD WORLD INTERIORS

1023 E. San Carlos Avenue • San Carlos, CA 94070
650-592-4200

When one upholsterer highly recommends another, it's time to pay attention! That's how I first heard about Gerald De Julio, the award-winning owner of Old World Interiors since 1970. The interesting thing is, Gerry started out doing auto upholstery, and now specializes in re-upholstery of antique and European furniture. Open Monday through Friday 9 to 5 and Saturday 10 to 4.

RAFAEL INTERIORS
150 Mitchell Blvd #260 • San Rafael, CA 94903
415-492-8636

Simon Eilenkrig trained in Kiev in the art of antique restoration
and worked for two leading San Francisco upholsterers before
opening his own business in 1992. He welcomes very challenging
projects that other upholsterers pass on, like heavily tufted Victorian pieces stuffed with horsehair and covered in leather. He
builds mattresses from scratch the old-fashioned way with hand
tied coil springs and refers to one area of his workshop as "the
chicken house" where he hand constructs down cushions and pillows in any shape or size. Open 9 to 5 Monday through Friday.

RENAISSANCE FURNITURE RESTORATION
(See Furniture Refinishing, Restoration & Repair)

STUDIO TRICKEY
(See Window, Curtains & Draperies)

UPHOLSTERY CLEANING

GROMM RUG & UPHOLSTERY CLEANING
(See Carpet & Area Rug Cleaning)

WALLPAPER

DAKES INTERIORS

342 West Portal Avenue • San Francisco, CA 94127
415-665-9200

Did you know that it is virtually impossible to purchase wallpaper anywhere in San Francisco without an interior decorator? Except for one place—Dakes Interiors! They stock hundreds of sample books, including Winfield, Thibout, Shoemacher, Waverly, Sanderson, Stroheim & Romann, Zoffany, Anaglypta, York, as well as grass cloth, cork, and rice papers. Samples are available to try at home. Good luck!

TAMALPAIS PAINT & COLOR INC.

30 Tamalpais Drive • Corte Madera, CA 94925 • 415-924-1928

This wonderful little paint store has been around since the 1970s and operates a busy wallpaper annex right next door. Joyce Bohlman (a.k.a., the "wallpaper queen") presides over three other full-time consultants. In addition to brand names like Ralph Lauren, Schumacher, Stroheim & Roman, Waverly, and Arté they also carry historical papers, grass cloth, and vinyl. Large samples to try at home can be ordered for a small fee and they are generous with referrals for reputable paperhangers, etc. Hours are Monday through Friday 6 to 6:30, Saturday 8 to 5 and Sunday 9 to 3.

WALLPAPER INSTALLATION

BILL EMBERTON
415-922-2733

Bill has been hanging wallpaper since 1971, and even after all these years he still enjoys his work—and it shows. Several years ago, one of Bill's rooms in a decorators' showcase house was featured in *Architectural Digest*, and it had fifteen different wallpapers!

BRIAN SULLIVAN
510-414-7595

In addition to paper, Brian enjoys the challenge of hanging linen and hand-trimmed, paper-backed fabrics like silk. Brian has developed a special technique for working with silk so that it doesn't stain during the hanging process. Brian's expertise makes him the man to call for any wallpaper emergency.

ELIZABETH JOHNSON
1414 Noriega #3 • San Francisco, CA 94122 • 415-681-5129

Elizabeth Johnson and her husband, Matthew Crane, focus on extremely specialized and difficult-to-hang wall coverings. Complex installation, including unusually textured or fragile coverings, murals, and computer-generated wallpaper. Elizabeth and Matthew have been in business since 1989.

GINGERBREAD
2269 Chestnut Street • San Francisco, CA 94123 • 415-673-4116

Kit Haskell was an art major in college and apprenticed with many fine paperhangers before she decided to go out on her own in 1990. She specializes in Anaglypta, an embossed paper used on ceilings and under wainscot, and Lincrusta, a sturdier, molded application, also used under wainscot and once commonly seen in Victorian hallways. She also does wall upholstery, trompe l'oeil, mural painting. Kit works all over the Bay Area and beyond.

HEIDI LAURENT WRIGHT

5659 Cabot Drive • Oakland, CA 94611

510-339-0884 • 510-541-9546 (cell)

Heidi started her career fresh out of college and has been at it since 1990. She feels she can hang nearly any wall material. One of her favorite jobs is repairing and restoring older wallpapers in historic homes and buildings. Heidi is a favorite with designers and contractors.

JILL STEVENS

730 Church Street #2 • San Francisco, CA 94114 • 415-255-8719

Jill is a much-in-demand paperhanger with an art history background who has been honing her craft since 1990. Her routine attention to detail and quest for perfection with every job impresses contractors and clients alike. Jill and her colleague are frequently asked to work not only all over California but out of state as well.

WALL UPHOLSTERY

FABRIC WALLS, INC.

322 Harriet Street • San Francisco, CA 94103

415-863-2711

In addition to expert wall upholstery installation, Don Piermarini and Ray Bollinger also custom fabricate curtains, window coverings, bedding, and pillows. Don and Ray do it all—measuring, manufacturing, and installation—whereas many workrooms outsource one or more of these services. Their exceptional attention to detail has created a demand for their talents all over the Bay Area as well as the Lake Tahoe area, Carmel and the wine country. Monday through Friday by appointment.

GINGERBREAD

(See Wallpaper Installation)

HANG IT UP TIM

P.O. Box 1391 • Burlingame, CA 94010 • 650-344-2642

Tim Spanier started his business in 1975 installing wall coverings, then upholstering walls and, following an inspirational trip to Italy, Venetian plasterwork. His understanding of color and love of texture enhance his special facility with this difficult medium. Tim works all over the Bay Area and travels for large commercial jobs. By appointment.

WATER DAMAGE RESTORATION

IDEAL DRYING

432 No. Canal Street #16 • San Francisco, CA 94080
1-800-379-6881 • www.ideal1.com

Ideal Drying has been taking care of flooding, leaking, and other water damage emergencies since 1973. Prompt response time and quick action minimize costly problems and prevent permanent damage from broken pipes, blocked drains, malfunctioning appliances, leaky roofs, and the like.

WINDOW BLIND INSTALLATION

DERRICK STUBBS

1757 Quincey Lane • Fairfield, CA 94534 • 415-726-9966

Derrick has been installing window blinds since 1980. More than twenty-five years of experience make him invaluable when it comes to measuring and trouble-shooting tricky jobs like awkward projections, stacking space, etc. But with Derrick on the job, you can be assured that your new window treatment will be a perfect fit. He works all over the Bay Area, including San Jose, Healdsburg, Sacramento, and Lake Tahoe.

WINDOW, CLEANING

CARLOS RAMIREZ WINDOW CLEANING

415 Buel Avenue • Pacifica, CA 94044

650-738-2794 • 650-219-3071 (cell)

www.windowcleaningsf.com

Carlos began working with his father at age fifteen on San Francisco high-rises and today is the third-generation owner of the family business. Servicing San Francisco and the Peninsula, rates are based on the type of cleaning needed and the number and style of windows.

CLASSIC WINDOW CLEANING

415-255-0950

While still in high school, Mike Donham learned the trade working with his dad. Mike enjoys the more challenging jobs, either commercial or residential, and works primarily in San Francisco, although occasionally he will go to other Bay Area locations. Mike charges by the job and is happy to come out and give you an estimate.

STREAKLESS WINDOW CLEANERS

415-509-6907

When Greg Thomas came to California from Connecticut in 1993 he knew it was where he wanted to live. Today, his residential window cleaning business has such a great reputation he does no advertising and gets all his work by referral—of which he is justifiably proud! Greg works only in Marin County by appointment.

THE WINDOW DOCTOR

Bryan Alberstat • 415-305-5327

Bryan is an experienced rock climber who often uses this skill to get him in and out of tight spots—an occupational hazard for window cleaners. When he needs extra help, Bryan hires a buddy from his climbing club! Bryan also does power washing for sidewalks, patios, home exteriors, etc. He prefers residential jobs in San Francisco, although loyal customers always seem to take him with them if they move out of the city. Bryan's fees are based primarily on window count. By appointment.

WINDOW, CURTAINS & DRAPERIES

ANGELIQUE'S INTERIORS
2346 B Marinship Way • Sausalito, CA 94103
415-339-0591 • Angelique@angeliqueinteriors.com

Angelique Clark started in the drapery business in 1990, but first she earned a degree in textiles and worked in the apparel industry. Angelique feels the use of refined dressmaker detailing sets her work apart, while computer technology also enables her to design a window treatment to scale, scan the client's fabric choices, and create a virtual product for approval. The location can be tricky to find so it's a good idea to call ahead for specific directions. And although someone is always there, you'll probably need an appointment to see Angelique. Open 8 to 4:30 Monday through Friday.

DREAMS
(See Pillow & Cushion Fabrication)

FABRIC WALLS, INC.
(See Wall Upholstery)

MAGNOLIA LANE
313 Corey Way • South San Francisco, CA 94080
650-624-0700

In 1980 Kathleen Redmond started a drapery business out of her home. About ten years ago, Riitta Herwitz came on board and today they provide top-quality soft home furnishings, including curtains, window shades and blinds, slipcovers, bedding and up-holstered headboards. Open Monday through Thursday 8 to 5 and Friday 8 to 3.

RIVERA'S DRAPERY SERVICE

6255 Mission Street • Daly City, CA 94014
650-991-4370

Since 1982 Maria Riviera has been doing all sewing and fabrica-tion while Jose Rivera has been responsible for the measuring and installation. This special partnership is held in high regard by their loyal clientele. They fabricate draperies, pillows, cornice boards and bedding. Hours are Monday through Thursday 8 to 4 and Saturday 8 to 3:30.

TRICKEY STUDIO

3320 18th Street • San Francisco, CA 94110
415-864-6516

In business since 1985, Robert Trickey provides every type of drapery service, including fabrication and installation of window blinds and Roman shades, as well as making custom slipcovers, decorative pillows, and upholstery or re-upholstery of bed frames and headboards. Copying sofas and chairs from existing pieces or a photo is another specialty. Open Monday through Friday 8:30 to 5:30.

WINDOW, ROMAN SHADES

THE ROMAN SHADE COMPANY

2 Henry Adams Street #341 • San Francisco, CA 94103
415-621-2777 • www.theromanshadecompany.com

Roman shades lend elegance to a room, and fortunately the mech-anisms have improved greatly since I started using them years ago. Nowadays they even come with motorized controls! They effective-ly control light as well as bringing a particular design sensibility to your windows. The Roman Shade Company, in business since 1992, provides expert design, product knowledge, and installation. Although located in the San Francisco Design Center, they are happy to work with the public as well as designers. Call for a consultation. Open Monday through Friday 10 to 5 or Saturday by appointment.

SMITH & NOBLE WINDOWARE
800-248-8888 • smithnoble.com

Most decorators don't use mail order companies for woven shades, but since it is extremely difficult to buy superior shades and blinds without a professional help, I thought I would include this find. In business since 1987, Smith & Noble makes the process fairly easy as the form in the catalog guides you through the measuring process. You can obtain swatches and advice by phone or online from their knowledgeable staff. If you are handy (and confident), doing the installation yourself is an economical alternative. Or, look under Window Blind Installation and hire them for the installation when your order arrives. Contact them for a catalog.

WOOD FLOORS, INSTALLATION & REFINISHING

PETER LAGOE "FLOORMAN"
415-389-5434

A self-described "down-sized engineer," Peter left the corporate world in 1992 to start his own company working with home and business owners, contractors and interior designers. He has flooring samples that he will bring to your home, including wood, vinyl and carpeting. Additionally, he refinishes wood flooring and makes repairs to carpeting. Peter prefers to work in San Francisco and in Marin County. Call him Monday to Friday 8 to 5.

RENAISSANCE FLOOR IN-LAYS

2159 Harbor Street • Pittsburg, CA 94565
925-427-6600 • www.hardwoodfloorandinlays.com

Marquetry flooring, once reserved for wealthy European nobility, is now being produced in this San Francisco workshop. In business since 1989, they have revived this specialized inlay technique, dating back to the Roman Empire, of inlaying shaped wood forms into wood of another species, usually in contrasting colors and grain. Renaissance Floor In-Lays offer 45 multidimensional patterns in the forms of medallions, panels, parquets, and borders. They manufacture and install these beautiful floors all over the world. Open Monday through Friday 8 to 4:30 and Saturday by appointment.

RODE BROTHERS

Larry Klosowski
10 Carolina Street • San Francisco, CA 94103
415-431-0457 • larry@rodebros.com

Rode Bros. has been installing custom hardwood flooring since 1930. Their clients have included the White House, the Getty Museum, the Peninsula Hotel in Beverly Hills, the Vintage Club in Indian Wells, and many other prominent locations. Used by contractors and interior designers worldwide, their specialty is customizing the size of the wood planking or parquet pattern to fit the room. Larry is usually in the showroom from 8 to 4 Monday through Friday, however it's always a good idea to call before stopping by.

TREE LOVERS FLOORS, INC.

664 Natoma Street • San Francisco, CA 94103
415-863-6833

Christopher Hildreth started Tree Lovers in 1972. The company has an EPA number and the staff feels their dedication to the environment plays a small, but important roll in the reduction of air pollution. But first and foremost, Tree Lovers provides the highest quality installation and finishing of hardwood floors using the finest craftsmanship available, including hand-sanding and distressing. Tree Lovers work all over the Bay Area as well as Mendocino, Modesto and the Monterey peninsula. Call them between 7 and 4 Monday through Friday.

A
B
C

D
E
F

G
H
I

J
K
L

M
N
O

P
Q
R